www.EffortlessMath.com

... So Much More Online!

✓ FREE Math lessons

✓ More Math learning books!

✓ Mathematics Worksheets

✓ Online Math Tutors

Need a PDF version of this book?

Visit www.EffortlessMath.com

TSI

Mathematics

Prep 2019

A Comprehensive Review and Ultimate Guide to the TSI Math Test

By

Reza Nazari & Ava Ross

All inquiries should be addressed to:

info@effortlessMath.com

www.EffortlessMath.com

ISBN: 9781728710976

Published by: Effortless Math Education

www.EffortlessMath.com

Description

TSI Mathematics Prep 2019 provides students with the confidence and math skills they need to succeed on the TSI Math, building a solid foundation of basic Math topics with abundant exercises for each topic. It is designed to address the needs of TSI test takers who must have a working knowledge of basic Math.

This comprehensive book with over 2,500 sample questions and 2 complete TSI tests is all you need to fully prepare for the TSI Math. It will help you learn everything you need to ace the math section of the TSI.

There are more than 2,500 Math problems with answers in this book.

Effortless Math unique study program provides you with an in-depth focus on the math portion of the exam, helping you master the math skills that students find the most troublesome.

This book contains most common sample questions that are most likely to appear in the mathematics section of the TSI.

Inside the pages of this comprehensive TSI Math book, students can learn basic math operations in a structured manner with a complete study program to help them understand essential math skills. It also has many exciting features, including:

- Dynamic design and easy-to-follow activities
- A fun, interactive and concrete learning process
- Targeted, skill-building practices
- Fun exercises that build confidence
- Math topics are grouped by category, so you can focus on the topics you struggle on
- All solutions for the exercises are included, so you will always find the answers
- 2 Complete TSI Math Practice Tests that reflect the format and question types on TSI

TSI Mathematical Reasoning Prep 2019 is an incredibly useful tool for those who want to review all topics being covered on the TSI test. It efficiently and effectively reinforces learning outcomes through engaging questions and repeated practice, helping you to quickly master basic Math skills.

About the Author

Reza Nazari is the author of more than 100 Math learning books including:
– **Math and Critical Thinking Challenges:** For the Middle and High School Student
– **ACT Math in 30 Days.**
– **ASVAB Math Workbook 2018 – 2019**
– **Effortless Math Education Workbooks**
– **and many more Mathematics books ...**

Reza is also an experienced Math instructor and a test–prep expert who has been tutoring students since 2008. Reza is the founder of Effortless Math Education, a tutoring company that has helped many students raise their standardized test scores—and attend the colleges of their dreams. Reza provides an individualized custom learning plan and the personalized attention that makes a difference in how students view math.

To ask questions about Math, you can contact Reza via email at:
reza@EffortlessMath.com

Find Reza's professional profile at:
goo.gl/zoC9rJ

Contents

Chapter 1: Fractions and Decimals

Topics that you'll learn in this chapter:

✓ Simplifying Fractions

✓ Adding and Subtracting Fractions

✓ Multiplying and Dividing Fractions

✓ Adding Mixed Numbers

✓ Subtract Mixed Numbers

✓ Multiplying Mixed Numbers

✓ Dividing Mixed Numbers

✓ Comparing Decimals

✓ Rounding Decimals

✓ Adding and Subtracting Decimals

✓ Multiplying and Dividing Decimals

✓ Converting Between Fractions, Decimals and Mixed Numbers

✓ Factoring Numbers

✓ Greatest Common Factor

✓ Least Common Multiple

✓ Divisibility Rules

"A Man is like a fraction whose numerator is what he is and whose denominator is what he thinks of himself. The larger the denominator, the smaller the fraction." –Tolstoy

Simplifying Fractions

Helpful Hints	– Evenly divide both the top and bottom of the fraction by 2, 3, 5, 7, ... etc. – Continue until you can't go any further.	Example: $\dfrac{4}{12} = \dfrac{2}{6} = \dfrac{1}{3}$

✎ *Simplify the fractions.*

1) $\dfrac{22}{36}$

2) $\dfrac{8}{10}$

3) $\dfrac{12}{18}$

4) $\dfrac{6}{8}$

5) $\dfrac{13}{39}$

6) $\dfrac{5}{20}$

7) $\dfrac{16}{36}$

8) $\dfrac{18}{36}$

9) $\dfrac{20}{50}$

10) $\dfrac{6}{54}$

11) $\dfrac{45}{81}$

12) $\dfrac{21}{28}$

13) $\dfrac{35}{56}$

14) $\dfrac{52}{64}$

15) $\dfrac{13}{65}$

16) $\dfrac{44}{77}$

17) $\dfrac{21}{42}$

18) $\dfrac{15}{36}$

19) $\dfrac{9}{24}$

20) $\dfrac{20}{80}$

21) $\dfrac{25}{45}$

Adding and Subtracting Fractions

Helpful

Hints

– For "like" fractions (fractions with the same denominator), add or subtract the numerators and write the answer over the common denominator.
– Find equivalent fractions with the same denominator before you can add or subtract fractions with different denominators.
– Adding and Subtracting with the same denominator:

$$\frac{a}{b} + \frac{c}{b} = \frac{a+c}{b}$$
$$\frac{a}{b} - \frac{c}{b} = \frac{a-c}{b}$$

– Adding and Subtracting fractions with different denominators:

$$\frac{a}{b} + \frac{c}{d} = \frac{ad+cb}{bd}$$
$$\frac{a}{b} - \frac{c}{d} = \frac{ad-cb}{bd}$$

✎ **Add fractions.**

1) $\frac{2}{3} + \frac{1}{2}$

2) $\frac{3}{5} + \frac{1}{3}$

3) $\frac{5}{6} + \frac{1}{2}$

4) $\frac{7}{4} + \frac{5}{9}$

5) $\frac{2}{5} + \frac{1}{5}$

6) $\frac{3}{7} + \frac{1}{2}$

7) $\frac{3}{4} + \frac{2}{5}$

8) $\frac{2}{3} + \frac{1}{5}$

9) $\frac{16}{25} + \frac{3}{5}$

✎ **Subtract fractions.**

10) $\frac{4}{5} - \frac{2}{5}$

11) $\frac{3}{5} - \frac{2}{7}$

12) $\frac{1}{2} - \frac{1}{3}$

13) $\frac{8}{9} - \frac{3}{5}$

14) $\frac{3}{7} - \frac{3}{14}$

15) $\frac{4}{15} - \frac{1}{10}$

16) $\frac{3}{4} - \frac{13}{18}$

17) $\frac{5}{8} - \frac{2}{5}$

18) $\frac{1}{2} - \frac{1}{9}$

Multiplying and Dividing Fractions

Helpful Hints	– **Multiplying fractions:** multiply the top numbers and multiply the bottom numbers. – **Dividing fractions:** Keep, Change, Flip Keep first fraction, change division sign to multiplication, and flip the numerator and denominator of the second fraction. Then, solve!	Example: $\dfrac{a}{b} \times \dfrac{c}{d} = \dfrac{a \times c}{b \times d}$ $\dfrac{a}{b} \div \dfrac{c}{d} = \dfrac{a}{b} \times \dfrac{d}{c} = \dfrac{ad}{bc}$

✎ *Multiplying fractions. Then simplify.*

1) $\dfrac{1}{5} \times \dfrac{2}{3}$

2) $\dfrac{3}{4} \times \dfrac{2}{3}$

3) $\dfrac{2}{5} \times \dfrac{3}{7}$

4) $\dfrac{3}{8} \times \dfrac{1}{3}$

5) $\dfrac{3}{5} \times \dfrac{2}{5}$

6) $\dfrac{7}{9} \times \dfrac{1}{3}$

7) $\dfrac{2}{3} \times \dfrac{3}{8}$

8) $\dfrac{1}{4} \times \dfrac{1}{3}$

9) $\dfrac{5}{7} \times \dfrac{7}{12}$

✎ *Dividing fractions.*

10) $\dfrac{2}{9} \div \dfrac{1}{4}$

11) $\dfrac{1}{2} \div \dfrac{1}{3}$

12) $\dfrac{6}{11} \div \dfrac{3}{4}$

13) $\dfrac{11}{14} \div \dfrac{1}{10}$

14) $\dfrac{3}{5} \div \dfrac{5}{9}$

15) $\dfrac{1}{2} \div \dfrac{1}{2}$

16) $\dfrac{3}{5} \div \dfrac{1}{5}$

17) $\dfrac{12}{21} \div \dfrac{3}{7}$

18) $\dfrac{5}{14} \div \dfrac{9}{10}$

Adding Mixed Numbers

Helpful **Hints**	Use the following steps for both adding and subtracting mixed numbers.	**Example:**
	– Find the Least Common Denominator (LCD) – Find the equivalent fractions for each mixed number. – Add fractions after finding common denominator. – Write your answer in lowest terms.	$1\frac{3}{4} + 2\frac{3}{8} = 4\frac{1}{8}$

✎ *Add.*

1) $4\frac{1}{2} + 5\frac{1}{2}$

2) $2\frac{3}{8} + 3\frac{1}{8}$

3) $6\frac{1}{5} + 3\frac{2}{5}$

4) $1\frac{1}{3} + 2\frac{2}{3}$

5) $5\frac{1}{6} + 5\frac{1}{2}$

6) $3\frac{1}{3} + 1\frac{1}{3}$

7) $1\frac{10}{11} + 1\frac{1}{3}$

8) $2\frac{3}{6} + 1\frac{1}{2}$

9) $5\frac{3}{5} + 5\frac{1}{5}$

10) $7 + \frac{1}{5}$

11) $1\frac{5}{7} + \frac{1}{3}$

12) $2\frac{1}{4} + 1\frac{1}{2}$

Subtract Mixed Numbers

Helpful	Use the following steps for both adding and subtracting mixed numbers.	**Example:**
Hints	Find the Least Common Denominator (LCD) – Find the equivalent fractions for each mixed number. – Add or subtract fractions after finding common denominator. – Write your answer in lowest terms.	$5\frac{2}{3} - 3\frac{2}{7} = 2\frac{8}{21}$

✎ *Subtract.*

1) $4\frac{1}{2} - 3\frac{1}{2}$

2) $3\frac{3}{8} - 3\frac{1}{8}$

3) $6\frac{3}{5} - 5\frac{1}{5}$

4) $2\frac{1}{3} - 1\frac{2}{3}$

5) $6\frac{1}{6} - 5\frac{1}{2}$

6) $3\frac{1}{3} - 1\frac{1}{3}$

7) $2\frac{10}{11} - 1\frac{1}{3}$

8) $2\frac{1}{2} - 1\frac{1}{2}$

9) $6\frac{3}{5} - 2\frac{1}{5}$

10) $7\frac{2}{5} - 1\frac{1}{5}$

11) $2\frac{5}{7} - 1\frac{1}{3}$

12) $2\frac{1}{4} - 1\frac{1}{2}$

Multiplying Mixed Numbers

Helpful	1- Convert the mixed numbers to improper fractions.	**Example:**

Helpful

Hints

1- Convert the mixed numbers to improper fractions.
2- Multiply fractions and simplify if necessary.

$$a\frac{c}{b} = a + \frac{c}{b} = \frac{ab+c}{b}$$

Example:

$$2\frac{1}{3} \times 5\frac{3}{7} =$$

$$\frac{7}{3} \times \frac{38}{7} = \frac{38}{3} = 12\frac{2}{3}$$

✎ *Find each product.*

1) $1\frac{2}{3} \times 1\frac{1}{4}$

2) $1\frac{3}{5} \times 1\frac{2}{3}$

3) $1\frac{2}{3} \times 3\frac{2}{7}$

4) $4\frac{1}{8} \times 1\frac{2}{5}$

5) $2\frac{2}{5} \times 3\frac{1}{5}$

6) $1\frac{1}{3} \times 1\frac{2}{3}$

7) $1\frac{5}{8} \times 2\frac{1}{2}$

8) $3\frac{2}{5} \times 2\frac{1}{5}$

9) $2\frac{2}{3} \times 4\frac{1}{4}$

10) $2\frac{3}{5} \times 1\frac{2}{4}$

11) $1\frac{1}{3} \times 1\frac{1}{4}$

12) $3\frac{2}{5} \times 1\frac{1}{5}$

Dividing Mixed Numbers

Helpful	1- Convert the mixed numbers to improper fractions.	**Example:**
Hints	2- Divide fractions and simplify if necessary.	$10\frac{1}{2} \div 5\frac{3}{5} =$

$$a\frac{c}{b} = a + \frac{c}{b} = \frac{ab+c}{b}$$

$$\frac{21}{2} \div \frac{28}{5} = \frac{21}{2} \times \frac{5}{28} = \frac{105}{56}$$

$$= 1\frac{7}{8}$$

✎ *Find each quotient.*

1) $2\frac{1}{5} \div 2\frac{1}{2}$

2) $2\frac{3}{5} \div 1\frac{1}{3}$

3) $3\frac{1}{6} \div 4\frac{2}{3}$

4) $1\frac{2}{3} \div 3\frac{1}{3}$

5) $4\frac{1}{8} \div 2\frac{2}{4}$

6) $3\frac{1}{2} \div 2\frac{3}{5}$

7) $3\frac{5}{9} \div 1\frac{2}{5}$

8) $2\frac{2}{7} \div 1\frac{1}{2}$

9) $3\frac{1}{5} \div 1\frac{1}{2}$

10) $4\frac{3}{5} \div 2\frac{1}{3}$

11) $6\frac{1}{6} \div 1\frac{2}{3}$

12) $2\frac{2}{3} \div 1\frac{1}{3}$

Comparing Decimals

Helpful	-	**Decimals:** is a fraction written in a special form. For example, instead of writing $\frac{1}{2}$ you can write 0.5.	**Example:**
Hints	-	**For comparing:** Equal to = Less than < Greater than > Greater than or equal ≥ Less than or equal ≤	2.67 > 0.267

✍ *Write the correct comparison symbol (>, < or =).*

1) 1.25   2.3

2) 0.5   0.23

3) 3.2   3.2

4) 4.58   45.8

5) 2.75   0.275

6) 5.2   5

7) 3.1   0.31

8) 6.33   0.733

9) 8   0.8

10) 4.56 0.456

11) 1.12 1.14

12) 2.77 2.78

13) 6.08 6.11

14) 1.11 0.211

15) 2.6   2.55

16) 1.24 1.25

17) 5.52 0.552

18) 0.33 0.033

19) 14.4 14.4

20) 0.05 0.50

21) 0.59 0.7

22) 0.5   0.05

23) 0.90 0.9

24) 0.27 0.4

Rounding Decimals

Helpful	We can round decimals to a certain accuracy or number of decimal places. This is used to make calculation easier to do and results easier to understand, when exact values are not too important.	**Example:**
Hints	First, you'll need to remember your place values:	$\underline{6}.37 = 6$

12.4567

1: tens	2: ones	4: tenths

5: hundredths	6: thousandths	7: tens thousandths

✍*Round each decimal number to the nearest place indicated.*

1) 0.2̲3	9) 1.6̲29	17) 70.7̲8
2) 4.0̲4	10) 6.3̲959	18) 615̲.755
3) 5.6̲23	11) 1̲.9	19) 16̲.4
4) 0.26̲6	12) 5̲.2167	20) 95̲.81
5) 6̲.37	13) 5.8̲63	21) 2̲.408
6) 0.8̲8	14) 8.5̲4	22) 76̲.3
7) 8.2̲4	15) 80̲.69	23) 116.5̲14
8) 7̲.0760	16) 65̲.85	24) 8.0̲6

Adding and Subtracting Decimals

Helpful	1– Line up the numbers.	**Example:**
	2– Add zeros to have same number of digits for both numbers.	
Hints	3– Add or Subtract using column addition or subtraction.	16.18 $- \; 13.45$ 2.73

✎ **Add and subtract decimals.**

1) 15.14 $- \; 12.18$ _____

2) 65.72 $+ \; 43.67$ _____

3) 82.56 $+ \; 12.28$ _____

4) 34.18 $- \; 23.45$ _____

5) 90.37 $+ \; 56.97$ _____

6) 45.78 $- \; 23.39$ _____

✎ **Solve.**

7) ____ + 1.3 = 4.8

8) 4.2 + ____ = 11.6

9) 9.9 + ____ = 16

10) 6.9 + ____ = 16.4

11) ____ + 5.1 = 8.6

12) ____ + 7.9 = 15.2

Multiplying and Dividing Decimals

Helpful

Hints

For Multiplication:

– Set up and multiply the numbers as you do with whole numbers.

– Count the total number of decimal places in both of the factors.

– Place the decimal point in the product.

For Division:

– If the divisor is not a whole number, move decimal point to right to make it a whole number. Do the same for dividend.

– Divide similar to whole numbers.

✍ **Find each product.**

1)
$$
\begin{array}{r}
4.5 \\
\times\ 1.6 \\
\hline
\end{array}
$$

2)
$$
\begin{array}{r}
7.7 \\
\times\ 9.9 \\
\hline
\end{array}
$$

3)
$$
\begin{array}{r}
2.6 \\
\times\ 1.5 \\
\hline
\end{array}
$$

4)
$$
\begin{array}{r}
8.9 \\
\times\ 9.7 \\
\hline
\end{array}
$$

5)
$$
\begin{array}{r}
15.1 \\
\times\ 12.6 \\
\hline
\end{array}
$$

6)
$$
\begin{array}{r}
6.9 \\
\times\ 3.3 \\
\hline
\end{array}
$$

7)
$$
\begin{array}{r}
5.7 \\
\times\ 7.8 \\
\hline
\end{array}
$$

8)
$$
\begin{array}{r}
98.20 \\
\times\ 100 \\
\hline
\end{array}
$$

9)
$$
\begin{array}{r}
23.99 \\
\times\ 1000 \\
\hline
\end{array}
$$

✍ **Find each quotient.**

10) $9.2 \div 3.6$

11) $27.6 \div 3.8$

12) $12.6 \div 4.7$

13) $6.5 \div 8.1$

14) $1.4 \div 10$

15) $3.6 \div 100$

16) $4.24 \div 10$

17) $14.6 \div 100$

18) $1.8 \div 1000$

Converting Between Fractions, Decimals and Mixed Numbers

Helpful *Hints*	**Fraction to Decimal:**
	– Divide the top number by the bottom number.
	Decimal to Fraction:
	– Write decimal over 1.
	– Multiply both top and bottom by 10 for every digit on the right side of the decimal point.
	– Simplify.

✎ *Convert fractions to decimals.*

1) $\dfrac{9}{10}$

2) $\dfrac{56}{100}$

3) $\dfrac{3}{4}$

4) $\dfrac{2}{5}$

5) $\dfrac{3}{9}$

6) $\dfrac{40}{50}$

7) $\dfrac{12}{10}$

8) $\dfrac{8}{5}$

9) $\dfrac{69}{10}$

✎ *Convert decimal into fraction or mixed numbers.*

10) 0.3

11) 4.5

12) 2.5

13) 2.3

14) 0.8

15) 0.25

16) 0.14

17) 0.2

18) 0.08

19) 0.45

20) 2.6

21) 5.2

Factoring Numbers

Helpful		- Factoring numbers means to break the numbers into their prime factors.	**Example:**
Hints		- First few prime numbers: 2, 3, 5, 7, 11, 13, 17, 19	$12 = 2 \times 2 \times 3$

✎ **List all positive factors of each number.**

1) 68

2) 56

3) 24

4) 40

5) 86

6) 78

7) 50

8) 98

9) 45

10) 26

11) 54

12) 28

13) 55

14) 85

15) 48

✎ **List the prime factorization for each number.**

16) 50

17) 25

18) 69

19) 21

20) 45

21) 68

22) 26

23) 86

24) 93

Greatest Common Factor

Helpful *Hints*	- List the prime factors of each number. - Multiply common prime factors.	**Example:** $200 = 2 \times 2 \times 2 \times 5 \times 5$ $60 = 2 \times 2 \times 3 \times 5$ GCF $(200, 60) = 2 \times 2 \times 5 = 20$

✎*Find the GCF for each number pair.*

1) 20, 30

2) 4, 14

3) 5, 45

4) 68, 12

5) 5, 12

6) 15, 27

7) 3, 24

8) 34, 6

9) 4, 10

10) 5, 3

11) 6, 16

12) 30, 3

13) 24, 28

14) 70, 10

15) 45, 8

16) 90, 35

17) 78, 34

18) 55, 75

19) 60, 72

20) 100, 78

21) 30, 40

Least Common Multiple

Helpful	- Find the GCF for the two numbers. - Divide that GCF into either number. - Take that answer and multiply it by the other number.	**Example:** LCM (200, 60): GCF is 20 $200 \div 20 = 10$ $10 \times 60 = 600$
Hints		

✎*Find the LCM for each number pair.*

1) 4, 14

2) 5, 15

3) 16, 10

4) 4, 34

5) 8, 3

6) 12, 24

7) 9, 18

8) 5, 6

9) 8, 19

10) 9, 21

11) 19, 29

12) 7, 6

13) 25, 6

14) 4, 8

15) 30, 10, 50

16) 18, 36, 27

17) 12, 8, 18

18) 8, 18, 4

19) 26, 20, 30

20) 10, 4, 24

21) 15, 30, 45

Answers of Worksheets – Chapter 1

Simplifying Fractions

1) $\dfrac{11}{18}$

2) $\dfrac{4}{5}$

3) $\dfrac{2}{3}$

4) $\dfrac{3}{4}$

5) $\dfrac{1}{3}$

6) $\dfrac{1}{4}$

7) $\dfrac{4}{9}$

8) $\dfrac{1}{2}$

9) $\dfrac{2}{5}$

10) $\dfrac{1}{9}$

11) $\dfrac{5}{9}$

12) $\dfrac{3}{4}$

13) $\dfrac{5}{8}$

14) $\dfrac{13}{16}$

15) $\dfrac{1}{5}$

16) $\dfrac{4}{7}$

17) $\dfrac{1}{2}$

18) $\dfrac{5}{12}$

19) $\dfrac{3}{8}$

20) $\dfrac{1}{4}$

21) $\dfrac{5}{9}$

Adding and Subtracting Fractions

1) $\dfrac{7}{6}$

2) $\dfrac{14}{15}$

3) $\dfrac{4}{3}$

4) $\dfrac{83}{36}$

5) $\dfrac{3}{5}$

6) $\dfrac{13}{14}$

7) $\dfrac{23}{20}$

8) $\dfrac{13}{15}$

9) $\dfrac{31}{25}$

10) $\dfrac{2}{5}$

11) $\dfrac{11}{35}$

12) $\dfrac{1}{6}$

13) $\dfrac{13}{45}$

14) $\dfrac{3}{14}$

15) $\dfrac{1}{6}$

16) $\dfrac{1}{36}$

17) $\dfrac{9}{40}$

18) $\dfrac{7}{18}$

Multiplying and Dividing Fractions

1) $\dfrac{2}{15}$

2) $\dfrac{1}{2}$

3) $\dfrac{6}{35}$

4) $\dfrac{1}{8}$

5) $\dfrac{6}{25}$

6) $\dfrac{7}{27}$

7) $\dfrac{1}{4}$

8) $\dfrac{1}{12}$

9) $\dfrac{5}{12}$

10) $\dfrac{8}{9}$

11) $\dfrac{3}{2}$

12) $\dfrac{8}{11}$

13) $\dfrac{55}{7}$

14) $\dfrac{27}{25}$

15) 1

16) 3

17) $\dfrac{4}{3}$

18) $\dfrac{25}{63}$

Adding Mixed Numbers

1) 10

2) $5\dfrac{1}{2}$

3) $9\dfrac{3}{5}$

4) 4

5) $10\dfrac{2}{3}$

6) $4\dfrac{2}{3}$

7) $3\dfrac{8}{33}$

8) 4

9) $10\dfrac{4}{5}$

10) $7\dfrac{1}{5}$

11) $2\dfrac{1}{21}$

12) $3\dfrac{3}{4}$

Subtract Mixed Numbers

1) 1

2) $\dfrac{1}{4}$

3) $1\dfrac{2}{5}$

4) $\dfrac{2}{3}$

5) $\dfrac{2}{3}$

6) 2

7) $1\dfrac{19}{33}$

8) 1

9) $4\dfrac{2}{5}$

10) $6\dfrac{1}{5}$

11) $1\dfrac{8}{21}$

12) $\dfrac{3}{4}$

Multiplying Mixed Numbers

1) $2\frac{1}{12}$

2) $2\frac{2}{3}$

3) $5\frac{10}{21}$

4) $5\frac{31}{40}$

5) $7\frac{17}{25}$

6) $2\frac{2}{9}$

7) $4\frac{1}{16}$

8) $7\frac{12}{25}$

9) $11\frac{1}{3}$

10) $3\frac{9}{10}$

11) $1\frac{2}{3}$

12) $4\frac{2}{25}$

Dividing Mixed Numbers

1) $\frac{22}{25}$

2) $1\frac{19}{20}$

3) $\frac{19}{28}$

4) $\frac{1}{2}$

5) $1\frac{13}{20}$

6) $1\frac{9}{26}$

7) $2\frac{34}{63}$

8) $1\frac{11}{21}$

9) $2\frac{2}{15}$

10) $1\frac{34}{35}$

11) $3\frac{7}{10}$

12) 2

Comparing Decimals

1) 1.25 < 2.3

2) 0.5 > 0.23

3) 3.2 = 3.2

4) 4.58 < 45.8

5) 2.75 > 0.275

6) 5.2 > 5

7) 3.1 > 0.31

8) 6.33 > 0.733

9) 8 > 0.8

10) 4.56 > 0.456

11) 1.12 < 1.14

12) 2.77 < 2.78

13) 6.08 < 6.11

14) 1.11 > 0.211

15) 2.6 > 2.55

16) 1.24 < 1.25

17) 5.52 > 0.552

18) 0.33 > 0.033

19) 14.4 = 14.4

20) 0.05 < 0.50

21) 0.59 < 0.7

22) 0.5 > 0.05

23) 0.90 = 0.9

24) 0.27 < 0.4

Rounding Decimals

1) 0.2	9) 1.63	17) 70.8
2) 4.0	10) 6.4	18) 616
3) 5.6	11) 2	19) 16
4) 0.3	12) 5	20) 96
5) 6	13) 5.9	21) 2
6) 0.9	14) 8.5	22) 76
7) 8.2	15) 81	23) 116.5
8) 7	16) 66	24) 8.1

Adding and Subtracting Decimals

1) 2.96	5) 147.34	9) 6.1
2) 109.39	6) 22.39	10) 9.5
3) 94.84	7) 3.5	11) 3.5
4) 10.73	8) 7.4	12) 7.3

Multiplying and Dividing Decimals

1) 7.2	7) 44.46	13) 0.8024...
2) 76.23	8) 9820	14) 0.14
3) 3.9	9) 23990	15) 0.036
4) 86.33	10) 2.5555...	16) 0.424
5) 190.26	11) 7.2631...	17) 0.146
6) 22.77	12) 2.6808...	18) 0.0018

Converting Between Fractions, Decimals and Mixed Numbers

1) 0.9	7) 1.2	12) $2\frac{1}{2}$
2) 0.56	8) 1.6	
3) 0.75	9) 6.9	13) $2\frac{3}{10}$
4) 0.4	10) $\frac{3}{10}$	14) $\frac{4}{5}$
5) 0.333...		
6) 0.8	11) $4\frac{1}{2}$	15) $\frac{1}{4}$

16) $\dfrac{7}{50}$ 18) $\dfrac{2}{25}$ 20) $2\dfrac{3}{5}$

17) $\dfrac{1}{5}$ 19) $\dfrac{9}{20}$ 21) $5\dfrac{1}{5}$

Factoring Numbers

1) 1, 2, 4, 17, 34, 68
2) 1, 2, 4, 7, 8, 14, 28, 56
3) 1, 2, 3, 4, 6, 8, 12, 24
4) 1, 2, 4, 5, 8, 10, 20, 40
5) 1, 2, 43, 86
6) 1, 2, 3, 6, 13, 26, 39, 78
7) 1, 2, 5, 10, 25, 50
8) 1, 2, 7, 14, 49, 98
9) 1, 3, 5, 9, 15, 45
10) 1, 2, 13, 26
11) 1, 2, 3, 6, 9, 18, 27, 54
12) 1, 2, 4, 7, 14, 28

13) 1, 5, 11, 55
14) 1, 5, 17, 85
15) 1, 2, 3, 4, 6, 8, 12, 16, 24, 48
16) $2 \times 5 \times 5$
17) 5×5
18) 3×23
19) 3×7
20) $3 \times 3 \times 5$
21) $2 \times 2 \times 17$
22) 2×13
23) 2×43
24) 3×31

Greatest Common Factor

1) 10
2) 2
3) 5
4) 4
5) 1
6) 3
7) 3

8) 2
9) 2
10) 1
11) 2
12) 3
13) 4
14) 10

15) 1
16) 5
17) 2
18) 5
19) 12
20) 2
21) 10

Least Common Multiple

1) 28
2) 15
3) 80
4) 68
5) 24
6) 24
7) 18

8) 30
9) 152
10) 63
11) 551
12) 42
13) 150
14) 8

15) 150
16) 108
17) 72
18) 72
19) 780
20) 120

90

Chapter 2: Real Numbers and Integers

Topics that you'll learn in this chapter:

- ✓ Adding and Subtracting Integers
- ✓ Multiplying and Dividing Integers
- ✓ Ordering Integers and Numbers
- ✓ Arrange and Order, Comparing Integers
- ✓ Order of Operations
- ✓ Mixed Integer Computations
- ✓ Integers and Absolute Value

"Wherever there is number, there is beauty." –Proclus

Adding and Subtracting Integers

Helpful	-	**Integers:** {... , −3, −2, −1, 0, 1, 2, 3, ...} Includes: zero, counting numbers, and the negative of the counting numbers.	**Example:**
Hints		– Add a positive integer by moving to the right on the number line.	$12 + 10 = 22$ $25 − 13 = 12$
		– Add a negative integer by moving to the left on the number line.	$(−24) + 12 = −12$ $(−14) + (−12) = −26$
		– Subtract an integer by adding its opposite.	$14 − (−13) = 27$

✎ *Find the sum.*

1) $(− 12) + (− 4)$ 6) $(− 23) + (− 4) + 3$

2) $5 + (− 24)$ 7) $4 + (− 12) + (− 10) + (− 25)$

3) $(− 14) + 23$ 8) $19 + (− 15) + 25 + 11$

4) $(− 8) + (39)$ 9) $(− 9) + (− 12) + (32 − 14)$

5) $43 + (−12)$ 10) $4 + (− 30) + (45 − 34)$

✎ *Find the difference.*

11) $(− 14) − (− 9) − (18)$ 16) $(55) − (− 5) + (− 4)$

12) $(− 9) − (− 25)$ 17) $(9) − (2) − (− 5)$

13) $(− 12) − (8)$ 18) $(2) − (4) − (− 15)$

14) $(28) − (− 4)$ 19) $(23) − (4) − (− 34)$

15) $(34) − (2)$ 20) $(− 45) − (− 87)$

Multiplying and Dividing Integers

Helpful	(negative) × (negative) = positive	**Examples:**
	(negative) ÷ (negative) = positive	$3 \times 2 = 6$
Hints	(negative) × (positive) = negative	$3 \times -3 = -9$
	(negative) ÷ (positive) = negative	$-2 \times -2 = 4$
	(positive) × (positive) = positive	$10 \div 2 = 5$
		$-4 \div 2 = -2$
		$-12 \div -6 = 3$

✎ **Find each product.**

1) $(-8) \times (-2)$

2) 3×6

3) $(-4) \times 5 \times (-6)$

4) $2 \times (-6) \times (-6)$

5) $11 \times (-12)$

6) $10 \times (-5)$

7) 8×8

8) $(-8) \times (-9)$

9) $6 \times (-5) \times 3$

10) $6 \times (-1) \times 2$

✎ **Find each quotient.**

11) $18 \div 3$

12) $(-24) \div 4$

13) $(-63) \div (-9)$

14) $54 \div 9$

15) $20 \div (-2)$

16) $(-66) \div (-11)$

17) $64 \div 8$

18) $(-121) \div 11$

19) $72 \div 9$

20) $16 \div 4$

Ordering Integers and Numbers

Helpful *Hints*	To compare numbers, you can use number line! as you move from left to right on the number line, you find a bigger number!	**Example:** Order integers from least to greatest. $(-11, -13, 7, -2, 12)$ $-13 < -11 < -2 < 7 < 12$

✎ **Order each set of integers from least to greatest.**

1) $-15, -19, 20, -4, 1$ ___, ___, ___, ___, ___, ___

2) $6, -5, 4, -3, 2$ ___, ___, ___, ___, ___, ___

3) $15, -42, 19, 0, -22$ ___, ___, ___, ___, ___, ___

4) $26, -91, 0, -13, 67, -55$ ___, ___, ___, ___, ___, ___

5) $-17, -71, 90, -25, -54, -39$ ___, ___, ___, ___, ___, ___

6) $98, 5, 46, 19, 77, 24$ ___, ___, ___, ___, ___, ___

✎ **Order each set of integers from greatest to least.**

7) $-2, 5, -3, 6, -4$ ___, ___, ___, ___, ___, ___

8) $-37, 7, -17, 27, 47$ ___, ___, ___, ___, ___, ___

9) $32, -27, 19, -17, 15$ ___, ___, ___, ___, ___, ___

10) $68, 81, 21, -18, 94, 72$ ___, ___, ___, ___, ___, ___

Arrange, Order, and Comparing Integers

Helpful *Hints*	When using a number line, numbers increase as you move to the right.	**Examples:** $5 < 7,$ $-5 < -2$ $-18 < -12$

✎*Arrange these integers in descending order.*

1) $21, 71, -18, -10, 82$ ___, ___, ___, ___, ___, ___

2) $15, 11, 20, 12, -9, -5$ ___, ___, ___, ___, ___, ___

3) $-5, 20, 15, 9, -11$ ___, ___, ___, ___, ___, ___

4) $19, 18, -9, -6, -11$ ___, ___, ___, ___, ___, ___

5) $56, -34, -12, -5, 32$ ___, ___, ___, ___, ___, ___

✎*Compare. Use >, =, <*

6) -8 ____ 12 11) -56 ____ -58

7) -10 ____ -16 12) 78 ____ 87

8) 43 ____ 34 13) -92 ____ -102

9) 15 ____ -16 14) -12 ____ -12

10) -354 ____ -345 15) -721 ____ -821

Order of Operations

Helpful	-	Use "order of operations" rule when there are more than one math operation.	**Example:**
Hints	-	PEMDAS (parentheses / exponents / multiply / divide / add / subtract)	$(12 + 4) \div (-4) = -4$

✎ *Evaluate each expression.*

1) $(2 \times 2) + 5$

2) $24 - (3 \times 3)$

3) $(6 \times 4) + 8$

4) $25 - (4 \times 2)$

5) $(6 \times 5) + 3$

6) $64 - (2 \times 4)$

7) $25 + (1 \times 8)$

8) $(6 \times 7) + 7$

9) $48 \div (4 + 4)$

10) $(7 + 11) \div (-2)$

11) $9 + (2 \times 5) + 10$

12) $(5 + 8) \times \dfrac{3}{5} + 2$

13) $2 \times 7 - (\dfrac{10}{9 - 4})$

14) $(12 + 2 - 5) \times 7 - 1$

15) $(\dfrac{7}{5 - 1}) \times (2 + 6) \times 2$

16) $20 \div (4 - (10 - 8))$

17) $\dfrac{50}{4(5 - 4) - 3}$

18) $2 + (8 \times 2)$

Mixed Integer Computations

Helpful *Hints*	**It worth remembering:** (negative) × (negative) = positive (negative) ÷ (negative) = positive (negative) × (positive) = negative (negative) ÷ (positive) = negative (positive) × (positive) = positive	**Example:** $(-5) + 6 = 1$ $(-3) \times (-2) = 6$ $(9) \div (-3) = -3$

✎ *Compute.*

1) $(-70) \div (-5)$

2) $(-14) \times 3$

3) $(-4) \times (-15)$

4) $(-65) \div 5$

5) $18 \times (-7)$

6) $(-12) \times (-2)$

7) $\dfrac{(-60)}{(-20)}$

8) $24 \div (-8)$

9) $22 \div (-11)$

10) $\dfrac{(-27)}{3}$

11) $4 \times (-4)$

12) $\dfrac{(-48)}{12}$

13) $(-14) \times (-2)$

14) $(-7) \times (7)$

15) $\dfrac{-30}{-6}$

16) $(-54) \div 6$

17) $(-60) \div (-5)$

18) $(-7) \times (-12)$

19) $(-14) \times 5$

20) $88 \div (-8)$

Integers and Absolute Value

Helpful *Hints*	To find an absolute value of a number, just find it's distance from 0!	**Example:** $\|-6\| = 6$ $\|6\| = 6$ $\|-12\| = 12$ $\|12\| = 12$

✎ **Write absolute value of each number.**

1) − 4

2) − 7

3) − 8

4) 4

5) 5

6) − 10

7) 1

8) 6

9) 8

10) − 2

11) − 1

12) 10

13) 3

14) 7

15) − 5

16) − 3

17) − 9

18) 2

19) 4

20) − 6

21) 9

✎ **Evaluate.**

22) $\|-43\| - \|12\| + 10$

23) $76 + \|-15 - 45\| - \|3\|$

24) $30 + \|-62\| - 46$

25) $\|32\| - \|-78\| + 90$

26) $\|-35 + 4\| + 6 - 4$

27) $\|-4\| + \|-11\|$

28) $\|-6 + 3 - 4\| + \|7 + 7\|$

29) $\|-9\| + \|-19\| - 5$

Answers of Worksheets – Chapter 2

Adding and Subtracting Integers

1) − 16
2) − 19
3) 9
4) 31
5) 31
6) − 24
7) − 43

8) 40
9) − 3
10) − 15
11) − 23
12) 16
13) − 20
14) 32

15) 32
16) 56
17) 12
18) 13
19) 53
20) 42

Multiplying and Dividing Integers

1) 16
2) 18
3) 120
4) 72
5) − 132
6) − 50
7) 64

8) 72
9) − 90
10) − 12
11) 6
12) − 6
13) 7
14) 6

15) − 10
16) 6
17) 8
18) − 11
19) 8
20) 4

Ordering Integers and Numbers

1) − 19, − 15, − 4, 1, 20
2) − 5, − 3, 2, 4, 6
3) − 42, − 22, 0, 15, 19
4) − 91, − 55, − 13, 0, 26, 67
5) − 71, − 54, − 39, − 25, − 17, 90

6) 5, 19, 24, 46, 77, 98
7) 6, 5, − 2, − 3, − 4
8) 47, 27, 7, − 17, − 37
9) 32, 19, 15, − 17, − 27
10) 94, 81, 72, 68, 21, − 18

Arrange and Order, Comparing Integers

1) 82, 71, 21, − 10, − 18

2) 20, 15, 12, 11, − 5, − 9

3) 20, 15, 9, − 5, −11

4) 19, 18, − 6, − 9, − 11

5) 56, 32, − 5, − 12, − 34

6) <

7) >

8) >

9) >

10) <

11) >

12) <

13) >

14) =

15) >

Order of Operations

1) 9

2) 15

3) 32

4) 17

5) 33

6) 56

7) 33

8) 49

9) 6

10) − 9

11) 29

12) 9.8

13) 12

14) 62

15) 28

16) 10

17) 50

18) 18

Mixed Integer Computations

1) 14

2) − 42

3) 60

4) − 13

5) − 126

6) 24

7) 3

8) − 3

9) − 2

10) − 9

11) − 16

12) − 4

13) 28

14) − 49

15) 5

16) − 9

17) 12

18) 84

19) − 70

20) − 11

Integers and Absolute Value

1) 4
2) 7
3) 8
4) 4
5) 5
6) 10
7) 1
8) 6
9) 8
10) 2

11) 1
12) 10
13) 3
14) 7
15) 5
16) 3
17) 9
18) 2
19) 4
20) 6

21) 9
22) 41
23) 133
24) 46
25) 44
26) 33
27) 15
28) 21
29) 23

Chapter 3: Proportions and Ratios

Topics that you'll learn in this chapter:

- ✓ Writing Ratios
- ✓ Simplifying Ratios
- ✓ Create a Proportion
- ✓ Similar Figures
- ✓ Simple Interest
- ✓ Ratio and Rates Word Problems

"Do not worry about your difficulties in mathematics. I can assure you mine are still greater." – Albert Einstein

Writing Ratios

Helpful Hints	– A ratio is a comparison of two numbers. Ratio can be written as a division.	Example: $3:5$, or $\frac{3}{5}$

✍ **Express each ratio as a rate and unite rate.**

1) 120 miles on 4 gallons of gas.

2) 24 dollars for 6 books.

3) 200 miles on 14 gallons of gas

4) 24 inches of snow in 8 hours

✍ **Express each ratio as a fraction in the simplest form.**

5) 3 feet out of 30 feet

6) 18 cakes out of 42 cakes

7) 16 dimes t0 24 dimes

8) 12 dimes out of 48 coins

9) 14 cups to 84 cups

10) 45 gallons to 65 gallons

11) 10 miles out of 40 miles

12) 22 blue cars out of 55 cars

13) 32 pennies to 300 pennies

14) 24 beetles out of 86 insects

Simplifying Ratios

Helpful *Hints*	– You can calculate equivalent ratios by multiplying or dividing both sides of the ratio by the same number.	**Examples:**
		$3 : 6 = 1 : 2$
		$4 : 9 = 8 : 18$

✍ *Reduce each ratio.*

1) $21 : 49$

2) $20 : 40$

3) $10 : 50$

4) $14 : 18$

5) $45 : 27$

6) $49 : 21$

7) $100 : 10$

8) $12 : 8$

9) $35 : 45$

10) $8 : 20$

11) $25 : 35$

12) $21 : 27$

13) $52 : 82$

14) $12 : 36$

15) $24 : 3$

16) $15 : 30$

17) $3 : 36$

18) $8 : 16$

19) $6 : 100$

20) $2 : 20$

21) $10 : 60$

22) $14 : 63$

23) $68 : 80$

24) $8 : 80$

Create a Proportion

Helpful	— A proportion contains 2 equal fractions! A proportion simply means that two fractions are equal.	Example:
Hints		2, 4, 8, 16
		$\dfrac{2}{4} = \dfrac{8}{16}$

✎ *Create proportion from the given set of numbers.*

1) 1, 6, 2, 3

2) 12, 144, 1, 12

3) 16, 4, 8, 2

4) 9, 5, 27, 15

5) 7, 10, 60, 42

6) 8, 7, 24, 21

7) 10, 5, 8, 4

8) 3, 12, 8, 2

9) 2, 2, 1, 4

10) 3, 6, 7, 14

11) 2, 6, 5, 15

12) 7, 2, 14, 4

Similar Figures

Helpful Hints	– Two or more figures are similar if the corresponding angles are equal, and the corresponding sides are in proportion.	**Example:** 3–4–5 triangle is similar to a 6–8–10 triangle

✐ *Each pair of figures is similar. Find the missing side.*

1)

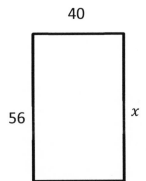
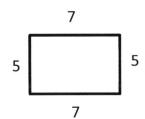

2)

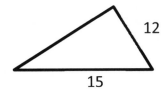
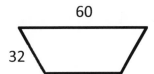

3)

Simple Interest

Helpful *Hints*	**Simple Interest:** The charge for borrowing money or the return for lending it. Interest = principal x rate x time $$I = prt$$	**Example:** $450 at 7% for 8 years. $$I = prt$$ $$I = 450 \times 0.07 \times 8 = \$252 =$$

✍ Use simple interest to find the ending balance.

1) $1,300 at 5% for 6 years.

2) $5,400 at 7.5% for 6 months.

3) $25,600 at 9.2% for 5 years

4) $24,000 at 8.5% for 9 years.

5) $450 at 7% for 8 years.

6) $54,200 at 8% for 5 years.

7) $240 interest is earned on a principal of $1500 at a simple interest rate of 4% interest per year. For how many years was the principal invested?

8) A new car, valued at $28,000, depreciates at 9% per year from original price. Find the value of the car 3 years after purchase.

9) Sara puts $2,000 into an investment yielding 5% annual simple interest; she left the money in for five years. How much interest does Sara get at the end of those five years?

Ratio and Rates Word Problems

Helpful *Hints*	To solve a ratio or a rate word problem, create a proportion and use cross multiplication method!	**Example:** $\dfrac{x}{4} = \dfrac{8}{16}$ $16x = 4 \times 8$ $x = 2$

✎**Solve.**

1) In a party, 10 soft drinks are required for every 12 guests. If there are 252 guests, how many soft drink is required?

2) In Jack's class, 18 of the students are tall and 10 are short. In Michael's class 54 students are tall and 30 students are short. Which class has a higher ratio of tall to short students?

3) Are these ratios equivalent?

   12 cards to 72 animals 11 marbles to 66 marbles

4) The price of 3 apples at the Quick Market is $1.44. The price of 5 of the same apples at Walmart is $2.50. Which place is the better buy?

5) The bakers at a Bakery can make 160 bagels in 4 hours. How many bagels can they bake in 16 hours? What is that rate per hour?

6) You can buy 5 cans of green beans at a supermarket for $3.40. How much does it cost to buy 35 cans of green beans?

Answers of Worksheets – Chapter 3

Writing Ratios

1) $\frac{120\ miles}{4\ gallons}$, 30 miles per gallon

2) $\frac{24\ dollars}{6\ books}$, 4.00 dollars per book

3) $\frac{200\ miles}{14\ gallons}$, 14.29 miles per gallon

4) $\frac{24"\ of\ snow}{8\ hours}$, 3 inches of snow per hour

5) $\frac{1}{10}$

6) $\frac{3}{7}$

7) $\frac{2}{3}$

8) $\frac{1}{4}$

9) $\frac{1}{6}$

10) $\frac{9}{13}$

11) $\frac{1}{4}$

12) $\frac{2}{5}$

13) $\frac{8}{75}$

14) $\frac{12}{43}$

Simplifying Ratios

1) 3 : 7
2) 1 : 2
3) 1 : 5
4) 7 : 9
5) 5 : 3
6) 7 : 3
7) 10 : 1
8) 3 : 2

9) 7 : 9
10) 2 : 5
11) 5 : 7
12) 7 : 9
13) 26 : 41
14) 1 : 3
15) 8 : 1
16) 1 : 2

17) 1 : 12
18) 1 : 2
19) 3 : 50
20) 1 : 10
21) 1: 6
22) 2 : 9
23) 17 : 20
24) 1 : 10

Create a Proportion

1) 1 : 3 = 2 : 6
2) 12 : 144 = 1 : 12
3) 2 : 4 = 8 : 16

4) 5 : 15 = 9 : 27
5) 7 : 42, 10 : 60
6) 7 : 21 = 8 : 24

7) 8 : 10 = 4 : 5
8) 2 : 3 = 8 : 12
9) 4 : 2 = 2 : 1

10) 7 : 3 = 14 : 6

11) 5 : 2 = 15 : 6

12) 7 : 2 = 14 : 4

Similar Figures

1) 5

2) 3

3) 56

Simple Interest

1) $1,690.00

2) $5,602.50

3) $37,376.00

4) $42,360.00

5) $702.00

6) $75,880.00

7) 4 years

8) $20,440

9) $500

Ratio and Rates Word Problems

1) 210

2) The ratio for both class is equal to 9 to 5.

3) Yes! Both ratios are 1 to 6

4) The price at the Quick Market is a better buy.

5) 640, the rate is 40 per hour.

6) $23.80

Chapter 4: Percent

Topics that you'll learn in this chapter:

- ✓ Percentage Calculations
- ✓ Converting Between Percent, Fractions, and Decimals
- ✓ Percent Problems
- ✓ Markup, Discount, and Tax

Mathematics - the unshaken Foundation of Sciences, and the plentiful Fountain of Advantage to human affairs. ~Isaac Barrow

Percentage Calculations

Helpful	-	Use the following formula to find part, whole, or percent:	**Example:**
Hints		$part = \dfrac{percent}{100} \times whole$	$\dfrac{20}{100} \times 100 = 20$

✎ *Calculate the percentages.*

1) 50% of 25

2) 80% of 15

3) 30% of 34

4) 70% of 45

5) 10% of 0

6) 80% of 22

7) 65% of 8

8) 78% of 54

9) 50% of 80

10) 20% of 10

11) 40% of 40

12) 90% of 0

13) 20% of 70

14) 55% of 60

15) 80% of 10

16) 20% of 880

17) 70% of 100

18) 80% of 90

✎ *Solve.*

19) 50 is what percentage of 75?

20) What percentage of 100 is 70

21) Find what percentage of 60 is 35.

22) 40 is what percentage of 80?

Converting Between Percent, Fractions, and Decimals

Helpful	– To a percent: Move the decimal point 2 places to the right and add the % symbol.	**Examples:**
Hints	– Divide by 100 to convert a number from percent to decimal.	30% = 0.3
		0.24 = 24%

✍ *Converting fractions to decimals.*

1) $\dfrac{50}{100}$ 4) $\dfrac{80}{100}$ 7) $\dfrac{90}{100}$

2) $\dfrac{38}{100}$ 5) $\dfrac{7}{100}$ 8) $\dfrac{20}{100}$

3) $\dfrac{15}{100}$ 6) $\dfrac{35}{100}$ 9) $\dfrac{7}{100}$

✍ *Write each decimal as a percent.*

10) 0.5   13) 0.524   16) 3.63

11) 0.9   14) 0.1   17) 0.008

12) 0.002   15) 0.03   18) 4.78

Percent Problems

Helpful *Hints*	Base = Part ÷ Percent Part = Percent × Base Percent = Part ÷ Base	**Example:** 2 is 10% of 20. 2 ÷ 0.10 = 20 2 = 0.10 × 20 0.10 = 2 ÷ 20

✎ *Solve each problem.*

1) 51 is 340% of what?

2) 93% of what number is 97?

3) 27% of 142 is what number?

4) What percent of 125 is 29.3?

5) 60 is what percent of 126?

6) 67 is 67% of what?

7) 67 is 13% of what?

8) 41% of 78 is what?

9) 1 is what percent of 52.6?

10) What is 59% of 14 m?

11) What is 90% of 130 inches?

12) 16 inches is 35% of what?

13) 90% of 54.4 hours is what?

14) What percent of 33.5 is 21?

15) Liam scored 22 out of 30 marks in Algebra, 35 out of 40 marks in science and 89 out of 100 marks in mathematics. In which subject his percentage of marks in best?

16) Ella require 50% to pass. If she gets 280 marks and falls short by 20 marks, what were the maximum marks she could have got?

Markup, Discount, and Tax

Helpful	-	**Markup** = selling price − cost Markup rate = markup divided by the cost	*Example:*
Hints	-	**Discount:** Multiply the regular price by the rate of discount Selling price = original price − discount	Original price of a microphone: $49.99, discount: 5%, tax: 5%
	-	**Tax:** To find tax, multiply the tax rate to the taxable amount (income, property value, etc.)	*Selling price = 49.87*

✎ *Find the selling price of each item.*

1) Cost of a pen: $1.95, markup: 70%, discount: 40%, tax: 5%

2) Cost of a puppy: $349.99, markup: 41%, discount: 23%

3) Cost of a shirt: $14.95, markup: 25%, discount: 45%

4) Cost of an oil change: $21.95, markup: 95%

5) Cost of computer: $1,850.00, markup: 75%

Answers of Worksheets – Chapter 4

Percentage Calculations

1) 12.5	9) 40	17) 70
2) 12	10) 2	18) 72
3) 10.2	11) 16	19) 67%
4) 31.5	12) 0	20) 70%
5) 0	13) 14	21) 58%
6) 17.6	14) 33	22) 50%
7) 5.2	15) 8	
8) 42.12	16) 176	

Converting Between Percent, Fractions, and Decimals

1) 0.5	7) 0.9	13) 52.4%
2) 0.38	8) 0.2	14) 10%
3) 0.15	9) 0.07	15) 3%
4) 0.8	10) 50%	16) 363%
5) 0.07	11) 90%	17) 0.8%
6) 0.35	12) 0.2%	18) 478%

Percent Problems

1) 15	7) 515.4	13) 49 hours
2) 104.3	8) 31.98	14) 62.7%
3) 38.34	9) 1.9%	15) Mathematics
4) 23.44%	10) 8.3 m	16) 600
5) 47.6%	11) 117 inches	
6) 100	12) 45.7 inches	

Markup, Discount, and Tax

1) $2.09
2) $379.98
3) $10.28
4) $36.22
5) $3,237.50

Chapter 5: Algebraic Expressions

Topics that you'll learn in this chapter:

- ✓ Expressions and Variables
- ✓ Simplifying Variable Expressions
- ✓ Simplifying Polynomial Expressions
- ✓ Translate Phrases into an Algebraic Statement
- ✓ The Distributive Property
- ✓ Evaluating One Variable
- ✓ Evaluating Two Variables
- ✓ Combining like Terms

Without mathematics, there's nothing you can do. Everything around you is mathematics. Everything around you is numbers." – Shakuntala Devi

Expressions and Variables

Helpful Hints	A variable is a letter that represents unknown numbers. A variable can be used in the same manner as all other numbers:		
	Addition	$2 + a$	2 plus a
	Subtraction	$y - 3$	y minus 3
	Division	$\dfrac{4}{x}$	4 divided by x
	Multiplication	$5a$	5 times a

✍ *Simplify each expression.*

1) $x + 5x$,

   use $x = 5$

2) $8\,(-3x + 9) + 6$,

   use $x = 6$

3) $10x - 2x + 6 - 5$,

   use $x = 5$

4) $2x - 3x - 9$,

   use $x = 7$

5) $(-6)\,(-2x - 4y)$,

   use $x = 1, y = 3$

6) $8x + 2 + 4\,y$,

   use $x = 9, y = 2$

7) $(-6)\,(-8x - 9y)$,

   use $x = 5, y = 5$

8) $6x + 5y$,

   use $x = 7, y = 4$

✍ *Simplify each expression.*

9) $5\,(-4 + 2x)$

10) $-3 - 5x - 6x + 9$

11) $6x - 3x - 8 + 10$

12) $(-8)\,(6x - 4) + 12$

13) $9\,(7x + 4) + 6x$

14) $(-9)\,(-5x + 2)$

Simplifying Variable Expressions

Helpful Hints	– Combine "like" terms. (values with same variable and same power) – Use distributive property if necessary. Distributive Property: $a(b + c) = ab + ac$	**Example:** $2x + 2(1 - 5x) =$ $2x + 2 - 10x = -8x + 2$

✎ *Simplify each expression.*

1) $-2 - x^2 - 6x^2$

2) $3 + 10x^2 + 2$

3) $8x^2 + 6x + 7x^2$

4) $5x^2 - 12x^2 + 8x$

5) $2x^2 - 2x - x$

6) $(-6)(8x - 4)$

7) $4x + 6(2 - 5x)$

8) $10x + 8(10x - 6)$

9) $9(-2x - 6) - 5$

10) $3(x + 9)$

11) $7x + 3 - 3x$

12) $2.5x^2 \times (-8x)$

✎ *Simplify.*

13) $-2(4 - 6x) - 3x$, $x = 1$

14) $2x + 8x$, $x = 2$

15) $9 - 2x + 5x + 2$, $x = 5$

16) $5(3x + 7)$, $x = 3$

17) $2(3 - 2x) - 4$, $x = 6$

18) $5x + 3x - 8$, $x = 3$

19) $x - 7x$, $x = 8$

20) $5(-2 - 9x)$, $x = 4$

Simplifying Polynomial Expressions

Helpful

Hints

- In mathematics, a polynomial is an expression consisting of variables and coefficients that involves only the operations of addition, subtraction, multiplication, and non–negative integer exponents of variables.

$$P(x) = a_0x^n + a_1x^{n-1} + \dots + a_{n-2}2x^2 + a_{n-1}x + a_n$$

Example:

An example of a polynomial of a single indeterminate x is

$x^2 - 4x + 7$.

An example for three variables is

$x^3 + 2xyz^2 - yz + 1$

✍ *Simplify each polynomial.*

1) $4x^5 - 5x^6 + 15x^5 - 12x^6 + 3\ x^6$

2) $(-3x^5 + 12 - 4x) + (8x^4 + 5x + 5\ x^5)$

3) $10x^2 - 5x^4 + 14x^3 - 20x^4 + 15x^3 - 8x^4$

4) $-6x^2 + 5x^2 - 7x^3 + 12 + 22$

5) $12x^5 - 5x^3 + 8x^2 - 8x^5$

6) $5x^3 + 1 + x^2 - 2x - 10x$

7) $14x^2 - 6x^3 - 2x\ (4x^2 + 2x)$

8) $(4x^4 - 2x) - (4x - 2x^4)$

9) $(3x^2 + 1) - (4 + 2x^2)$

10) $(2x + 2) - (7x + 6)$

11) $(12x^3 + 4x^4) - (2x^4 - 6x^3)$

12) $(12 + 3x^3) + (6x^3 + 6)$

13) $(5x^2 - 3) + (2x^2 - 3x^3)$

14) $(23x^3 - 12x^2) - (2x^2 - 9x^3)$

15) $(4x - 3x^3) - (3x^3 + 4x)$

Translate Phrases into an Algebraic Statement

Helpful *Hints*	**Translating key words and phrases into algebraic expressions:** **Addition:** plus, more than, the sum of, etc. **Subtraction:** minus, less than, decreased, etc. **Multiplication:** times, product, multiplied, etc. **Division:** quotient, divided, ratio, etc. **Example:** eight more than a number is 20 $8 + x = 20$

✎ *Write an algebraic expression for each phrase.*

1) A number increased by forty–two.

2) The sum of fifteen and a number

3) The difference between fifty–six and a number.

4) The quotient of thirty and a number.

5) Twice a number decreased by 25.

6) Four times the sum of a number and – 12.

7) A number divided by – 20.

8) The quotient of 60 and the product of a number and – 5.

9) Ten subtracted from a number.

10) The difference of six and a number.

The Distributive Property

Helpful

Hints

Distributive Property:

$$a(b + c) = ab + ac$$

Example:

$$3(4 + 3x)$$

$$= 12 + 9x$$

✎ **Use the distributive property to simply each expression.**

1) $-(-2 - 5x)$

2) $(-6x + 2)(-1)$

3) $(-5)(x - 2)$

4) $-(7 - 3x)$

5) $8(8 + 2x)$

6) $2(12 + 2x)$

7) $(-6x + 8)4$

8) $(3 - 6x)(-7)$

9) $(-12)(2x + 1)$

10) $(8 - 2x)9$

11) $(-2x)(-1 + 9x) - 4x(4 + 5x)$

12) $3(-5x - 3) + 4(6 - 3x)$

13) $(-2)(x + 4) - (2 + 3x)$

14) $(-4)(3x - 2) + 6(x + 1)$

15) $(-5)(4x - 1) + 4(x + 2)$

16) $(-3)(x + 4) - (2 + 3x)$

Evaluating One Variable

Helpful *Hints*	– To evaluate one variable expression, find the variable and substitute a number for that variable. – Perform the arithmetic operations.	**Example:** $4x + 8, x = 6$ $4(6) + 8 = 24 + 8 = 32$

✎ *Simplify each algebraic expression.*

1) $9 - x$, $x = 3$

2) $x + 2$, $x = 5$

3) $3x + 7$, $x = 6$

4) $x + (-5)$, $x = -2$

5) $3x + 6$, $x = 4$

6) $4x + 6$, $x = -1$

7) $10 + 2x - 6$, $x = 3$

8) $10 - 3x$, $x = 8$

9) $\dfrac{20}{x} - 3$, $x = 5$

10) $(-3) + \dfrac{x}{4} + 2x$, $x = 16$

11) $(-2) + \dfrac{x}{7}$, $x = 21$

12) $(-\dfrac{14}{x}) - 9 + 4x$, $x = 2$

13) $(-\dfrac{6}{x}) - 9 + 2x$, $x = 3$

14) $(-2) + \dfrac{x}{8}$, $x = 16$

Evaluating Two Variables

Helpful **Hints**	To evaluate an algebraic expression, substitute a number for each variable and perform the arithmetic operations.	**Example:** $2x + 4y - 3 + 2,$ $x = 5, y = 3$ $2(5) + 4(3) - 3 + 2$ $= 10$ $+ 12 - 3 + 2$ $= 21$

✎ *Simplify each algebraic expression.*

1) $2x + 4y - 3 + 2,$

   $x = 5, y = 3$

2) $(-\dfrac{12}{x}) + 1 + 5y,$

   $x = 6, y = 8$

3) $(-4)(-2a - 2b),$

   $a = 5, b = 3$

4) $10 + 3x + 7 - 2y,$

   $x = 7, y = 6$

5) $9x + 2 - 4y,$

   $x = 7, y = 5$

6) $6 + 3(-2x - 3y),$

   $x = 9, y = 7$

7) $12x + y,$

   $x = 4, y = 8$

8) $x \times 4 \div y,$

   $x = 3, y = 2$

9) $2x + 14 + 4y,$

   $x = 6, y = 8$

10) $4a - (5 - b),$

   $a = 4, b = 6$

Combining like Terms

Helpful *Hints*	– Terms are separated by "+" and "–" signs.	Example:
	– Like terms are terms with same variables and same powers.	$22x + 6 + 2x =$
	– Be sure to use the "+" or "–" that is in front of the coefficient.	$24x + 6$

✎*Simplify each expression.*

1) $5 + 2x - 8$

2) $(-2x + 6)\,2$

3) $7 + 3x + 6x - 4$

4) $(-4) - (3)(5x + 8)$

5) $9x - 7x - 5$

6) $x - 12x$

7) $7(3x + 6) + 2x$

8) $(-11x) - 10x$

9) $3x - 12 - 5x$

10) $13 + 4x - 5$

11) $(-22x) + 8x$

12) $2(4 + 3x) - 7x$

13) $(-4x) - (6 - 14x)$

14) $5(6x - 1) + 12x$

15) $22x + 6 + 2x$

16) $(-13x) - 14x$

17) $(-6x) - 9 + 15x$

18) $(-6x) + 7x$

19) $(-5x) + 12 + 7x$

20) $(-3x) - 9 + 15x$

21) $20x - 19x$

Answers of Worksheets – Chapter 5

Expressions and Variables

1) 30
2) −66
3) 41
4) −16
5) 84

6) 82
7) 510
8) 62
9) $10x − 20$
10) $6 − 11x$

11) $3x + 2$
12) $44 − 48x$
13) $69x + 36$
14) $45x − 18$

Simplifying Variable Expressions

1) $−7x^2 − 2$
2) $10x^2 + 5$
3) $15x^2 + 6x$
4) $−7x^2 + 8x$
5) $2x^2 − 3x$
6) $−48x + 24$
7) $−26x + 12$

8) $90x − 48$
9) $−18x − 59$
10) $3x + 27$
11) $4x + 3$
12) $−20x^3$
13) 1
14) 20

15) 26
16) 80
17) $−22$
18) 16
19) $−48$
20) $−190$

Simplifying Polynomial Expressions

1) $−14x^6 + 19x^5$
2) $2x^5 + 8x^4 + x + 12$
3) $−33x^4 + 29x^3 + 10x^2$
4) $−7x^3 − x^2 + 34$
5) $4x^5 − 5x^3 + 8x^2$
6) $5x^3 + x^2 − 12x + 1$
7) $−14x^3 + 10x^2$
8) $6x^4 − 6x$

9) $x^2 − 3$
10) $−5x − 4$
11) $2x^4 + 18x^3$
12) $9x^3 + 18$
13) $−3x^3 + 7x^2 − 3$
14) $32x^3 − 14x^2$
15) $−6x^3$

Translate Phrases into an Algebraic Statement

1) $x + 42$
3) $56 − x$
4) $30/x$
5) $2x − 25$
8) $\dfrac{60}{−5x}$

2) $15 + x$
6) $4(x + (−12))$
7) $\dfrac{x}{−20}$
9) $x − 10$
10) $6 − x$

The Distributive Property

1) $5x + 2$
2) $6x - 2$
3) $-5x + 10$
4) $3x - 7$
5) $16x + 64$
6) $4x + 24$

7) $-24x + 32$
8) $42x - 21$
9) $-24x - 12$
10) $-18x + 72$
11) $-38x^2 - 14x$
12) $-27x + 15$

13) $-5x - 10$
14) $-6x + 14$
15) $-16x + 13$
16) $-6x - 14$

Evaluating One Variable

1) 6
2) 7
3) 25
4) −7
5) 18

6) 2
7) 10
8) −14
9) 1
10) 33

11) 1
12) −8
13) −5
14) 0

Evaluating Two Variables

1) 21
2) 39
3) 64
4) 26

5) 45
6) −111
7) 56
8) 6

9) 58
10) 17

Combining like Terms

1) $2x - 3$
2) $-4x + 12$
3) $9x + 3$
4) $-15x - 28$
5) $2x - 5$
6) $-11x$
7) $23x + 42$

8) $-21x$
9) $-2x - 12$
10) $4x + 8$
11) $-14x$
12) $-x + 8$
13) $10x - 6$
14) $42x - 5$

15) $24x + 6$
16) $-27x$
17) $9x - 9$
18) x
19) $2x + 12$
20) $12x - 9$
21) x

Chapter 6: Equations

Topics that you'll learn in this chapter:

- ✓ One– Step Equations
- ✓ Two– Step Equations
- ✓ Multi– Step Equations

"The study of mathematics, like the Nile, begins in minuteness but ends in magnificence."

– Charles Caleb Colton

One–Step Equations

Helpful	-	The values of two expressions on both sides of an equation are equal. $$ax + b = c$$ - You only need to perform one Math operation in order to solve the equation.	**Example:** $-8x = 16$ $x = -2$
Hints			

✎ *Solve each equation.*

1) $x + 3 = 17$

2) $22 = (-8) + x$

3) $3x = (-30)$

4) $(-36) = (-6x)$

5) $(-6) = 4 + x$

6) $2 + x = (-2)$

7) $20x = (-220)$

8) $18 = x + 5$

9) $(-23) + x = (-19)$

10) $5x = (-45)$

11) $x - 12 = (-25)$

12) $x - 3 = (-12)$

13) $(-35) = x - 27$

14) $8 = 2x$

15) $(-6x) = 36$

16) $(-55) = (-5x)$

17) $x - 30 = 20$

18) $8x = 32$

19) $36 = (-4x)$

20) $4x = 68$

21) $30x = 300$

Two–Step Equations

Helpful	– You only need to perform two math operations (add, subtract, multiply, or divide) to solve the equation.	**Example:**
Hints	– Simplify using the inverse of addition or subtraction.	$-2(x-1) = 42$
	– Simplify further by using the inverse of multiplication or division.	$(x-1) = -21$
		$x = -20$

✎ *Solve each equation.*

1) $5(8 + x) = 20$

2) $(-7)(x - 9) = 42$

3) $(-12)(2x - 3) = (-12)$

4) $6(1 + x) = 12$

5) $12(2x + 4) = 60$

6) $7(3x + 2) = 42$

7) $8(14 + 2x) = (-34)$

8) $(-15)(2x - 4) = 48$

9) $3(x + 5) = 12$

10) $\dfrac{3x - 12}{6} = 4$

11) $(-12) = \dfrac{x + 15}{6}$

12) $110 = (-5)(2x - 6)$

13) $\dfrac{x}{8} - 12 = 4$

14) $20 = 12 + \dfrac{x}{4}$

15) $\dfrac{-24 + x}{6} = (-12)$

16) $(-4)(5 + 2x) = (-100)$

17) $(-12x) + 20 = 32$

18) $\dfrac{-2 + 6x}{4} = (-8)$

19) $\dfrac{x + 6}{5} = (-5)$

20) $(-9) + \dfrac{x}{4} = (-15)$

Multi–Step Equations

Helpful *Hints*	– Combine "like" terms on one side. – Bring variables to one side by adding or subtracting. – Simplify using the inverse of addition or subtraction. – Simplify further by using the inverse of multiplication or division.	**Example:** $3x + 15 = -2x + 5$ Add 2x both sides $5x + 15 = +5$ Subtract 15 both sides $5x = -10$ Divide by 5 both sides $x = -2$

✎ *Solve each equation.*

1) $-(2 - 2x) = 10$

2) $-12 = -(2x + 8)$

3) $3x + 15 = (-2x) + 5$

4) $-28 = (-2x) - 12x$

5) $2(1 + 2x) + 2x = -118$

6) $3x - 18 = 22 + x - 3 + x$

7) $12 - 2x = (-32) - x + x$

8) $7 - 3x - 3x = 3 - 3x$

9) $6 + 10x + 3x = (-30) + 4x$

10) $(-3x) - 8(-1 + 5x) = 352$

11) $24 = (-4x) - 8 + 8$

12) $9 = 2x - 7 + 6x$

13) $6(1 + 6x) = 294$

14) $-10 = (-4x) - 6x$

15) $4x - 2 = (-7) + 5x$

16) $5x - 14 = 8x + 4$

17) $40 = -(4x - 8)$

18) $(-18) - 6x = 6(1 + 3x)$

19) $x - 5 = -2(6 + 3x)$

20) $6 = 1 - 2x + 5$

Answers of Worksheets – Chapter 6

One–Step Equations

1) 14
2) 30
3) − 10
4) 6
5) − 10
6) − 4
7) − 11

8) 13
9) 4
10) − 9
11) − 13
12) − 9
13) − 8
14) 4

15) − 6
16) 11
17) 50
18) 4
19) − 9
20) 17
21) 10

Two–Step Equations

1) − 4
2) 3
3) 2
4) 1
5) 0.5
6) $\frac{4}{3}$
7) $-\frac{73}{8}$

8) $\frac{2}{5}$
9) − 1
10) 12
11) − 87
12) − 8
13) 128
14) 32

15) − 48
16) 10
17) − 1
18) − 5
19) − 31
20) − 24

Multi–Step Equations

1) 6
2) 2
3) − 2
4) 2
5) − 20
6) 37
7) 22

8) $\frac{4}{3}$
9) − 4
10) − 8
11) − 6
12) 2
13) 8

14) 1
15) 5
16) − 6
17) − 8
18) − 1
19) − 1
20) 0

Chapter 7: Inequalities

Topics that you'll learn in this chapter:

- ✓ Graphing Single– Variable Inequalities
- ✓ One– Step Inequalities
- ✓ Two– Step Inequalities
- ✓ Multi– Step Inequalities

Without mathematics, there's nothing you can do. Everything around you is mathematics. Everything around you is numbers." – Shakuntala Devi

Graphing Single–Variable Inequalities

Helpful *Hints*	– Isolate the variable.
	– Find the value of the inequality on the number line.
	– For less than or greater than draw open circle on the value of the variable.
	– If there is an equal sign too, then use filled circle.
	– Draw a line to the right direction.

✎ *Draw a graph for each inequality.*

1) $-2 > x$

2) $5 \leq -x$

3) $x > 7$

4) $-x > 1.5$

One–Step Inequalities

Helpful *Hints*	– Isolate the variable. – For dividing both sides by negative numbers, flip the direction of the inequality sign.	**Example:** $x + 4 \geq 11$ $x \geq 7$

✎ **Solve each inequality and graph it.**

1) $x + 9 \geq 11$

2) $x - 4 \leq 2$

3) $6x \geq 36$

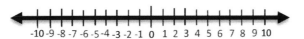

4) $7 + x < 16$

5) $x + 8 \leq 1$

6) $3x > 12$

7) $3x < 24$

Two–Step Inequalities

Helpful *Hints*	– Isolate the variable. – For dividing both sides by negative numbers, flip the direction of the of the inequality sign. – Simplify using the inverse of addition or subtraction. – Simplify further by using the inverse of multiplication or division.	**Example:** $2x + 9 \geq 11$ $2x \geq 2$ $x \geq 1$

✎ *Solve each inequality and graph it.*

1) $3x - 4 \leq 5$

2) $2x - 2 \leq 6$

3) $4x - 4 \leq 8$

4) $3x + 6 \geq 12$

5) $6x - 5 \geq 19$

6) $2x - 4 \leq 6$

7) $8x - 4 \leq 4$

8) $6x + 4 \leq 10$

9) $5x + 4 \leq 9$

10) $7x - 4 \leq 3$

11) $4x - 19 < 19$

12) $2x - 3 < 21$

13) $7 + 4x \geq 19$

14) $9 + 4x < 21$

15) $3 + 2x \geq 19$

16) $6 + 4x < 22$

Multi–Step Inequalities

Helpful *Hints*	– Isolate the variable. – Simplify using the inverse of addition or subtraction. – Simplify further by using the inverse of multiplication or division.	**Example:** $\dfrac{7x+1}{3} \geq 5$ $7x + 1 \geq 15$ $7x \geq 14$ $x \geq 7$

✍ *Solve each inequality.*

1) $\dfrac{9x}{7} - 7 < 2$

2) $\dfrac{4x + 8}{2} \leq 12$

3) $\dfrac{3x - 8}{7} > 1$

4) $-3\,(x - 7) > 21$

5) $4 + \dfrac{x}{3} < 7$

6) $\dfrac{2x + 6}{4} \leq 10$

Answers of Worksheets – Chapter 7

Graphing Single–Variable Inequalities

1) $-2 > x$

2) $x \leq -5$
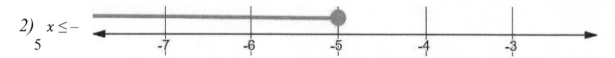

3) $x > 7$
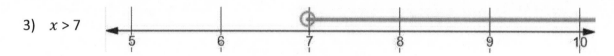

4) $-1.5 > x$
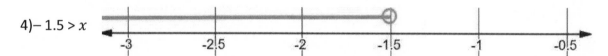

One–Step Inequalities

1)
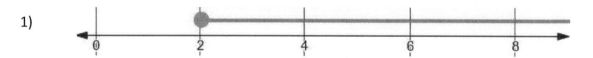

2)

3)
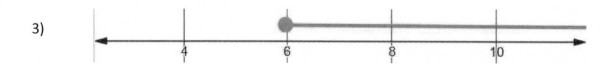

4)
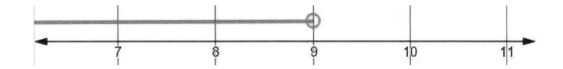

5)
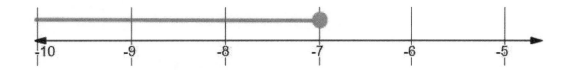

6)

7)

Two–Step inequalities

1) $x \leq 3$

2) $x \leq 4$

3) $x \leq 3$

4) $x \geq 2$

5) $x \geq 4$

6) $x \leq 5$

7) $x \leq 1$

8) $x \leq 1$

9) $x \leq 1$

10) $x \leq 1$

11) $x < 9.5$

12) $x < 12$

13) $x \geq 3$

14) $x < 3$

15) $x \geq 8$

16) $x < 4$

Multi–Step inequalities

1) $x < 7$

2) $x \leq 4$

3) $x > 5$

4) $x < 0$

5) $x < 9$

6) $x \leq 17$

Chapter 8: Linear Functions

Topics that you'll learn in this chapter:

- ✓ Finding Slope
- ✓ Graphing Lines Using Slope– Intercept Form
- ✓ Graphing Lines Using Standard Form
- ✓ Writing Linear Equations
- ✓ Graphing Linear Inequalities
- ✓ Finding Midpoint
- ✓ Finding Distance of Two Points

"Sometimes the questions are complicated and the answers are simple." – Dr. Seuss

Finding Slope

Helpful

Hints

Slope of a line:

$$\frac{y_2 - y_1}{x_2 - x_1} = \frac{rise}{run}$$

Example:

$(2, -10), (3, 6)$

slope = 16

✎ **Find the slope of the line through each pair of points.**

1) $(1, 1), (3, 5)$

2) $(4, -6), (-3, -8)$

3) $(7, -12), (5, 10)$

4) $(19, 3), (20, 3)$

5) $(15, 8), (-17, 9)$

6) $(6, -12), (15, -3)$

7) $(3, 1), (7, -5)$

8) $(3, -2), (-7, 8)$

9) $(15, -3), (-9, 5)$

10) $(-4, 7), (-6, -4)$

11) $(6, -8), (-11, -7)$

12) $(-6, 13), (17, -9)$

13) $(-10, -2), (-6, -5)$

14) $(4, 5), (-4, 10)$

15) $(-3, 1), (-17, 2)$

16) $(7, 0), (-13, -11)$

17) $(17, -13), (17, 8)$

18) $(12, 2), (-7, 5)$

Graphing Lines Using Slope–Intercept Form

Helpful	**Slope–intercept form:** given the slope m and the y–intercept b, then the equation of the line is:
Hints	$y = mx + b$.

Example:

$y = 8x - 3$

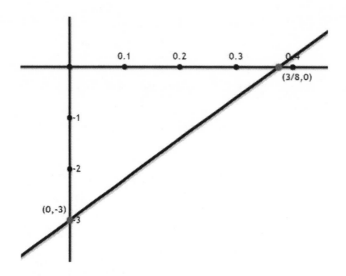

✎ **Sketch the graph of each line.**

1) $y = \dfrac{1}{2} x - 4$

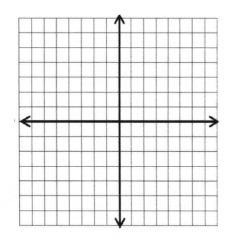

2) $y = 2x$

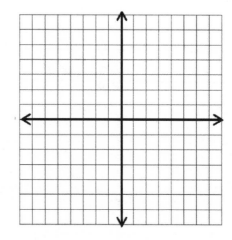

Graphing Lines Using Standard Form

Helpful	– Find the –intercept of the line by putting zero for y.
Hints	– Find the y–intercept of the line by putting zero for the x.
	– Connect these two points.

Example:

$x + 4y = 12$

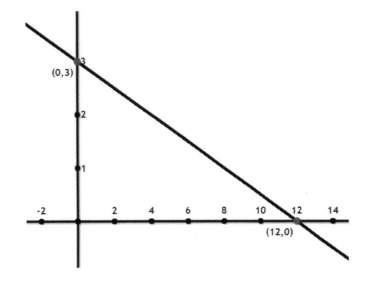

(0,3)

(12,0)

✎ **Sketch the graph of each line.**

1) $2x - y = 4$

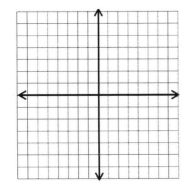

2) $x + y = 2$

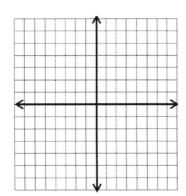

Writing Linear Equations

Helpful Hints	The equation of a line: $$y = mx + b$$ 1– Identify the slope. 2– Find the y–intercept. This can be done by substituting the slope and the coordinates of a point (x, y) on the line.	Example: through: $(-4, -2), (-3, 5)$ $y = 7x + 26$

✎ *Write the slope–intercept form of the equation of the line through the given points.*

1) through: $(-4, -2), (-3, 5)$

2) through: $(5, 4), (-4, 3)$

3) through: $(0, -2), (-5, 3)$

4) through: $(-1, 1), (-2, 6)$

5) through: $(0, 3), (-4, -1)$

6) through: $(0, 2), (1, -3)$

7) through: $(0, -5), (4, 3)$

8) through: $(-1, 4), (0, 4)$

9) through: $(2, -3), (3, -5)$

10) through: $(2, 5), (-1, -4)$

11) through: $(1, -3), (-3, 1)$

12) through: $(3, 3), (1, -5)$

13) through: $(4, 4), (3, -5)$

14) through: $(0, 3), (1, 1)$

15) through: $(5, 5), (2, -3)$

16) through: $(-2, -2), (2, -5)$

17) through: $(-3, -2), (1, -1)$

18) through: $(-2, 1), (6, 5)$

Graphing Linear Inequalities

Helpful

Hints

1– First, graph the "equals" line.

2– Choose a testing point. (it can be any point on both sides of the line.)

3– Put the value of (x, y) of that point in the inequality. If that works, that part of the line is the solution. If the values don't work, then the other part of the line is the solution.

✎*Sketch the graph of each linear inequality.*

1) $y < -4x + 2$

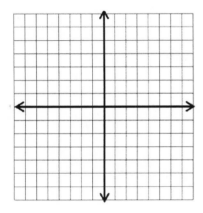

2) $2x + y < -4$

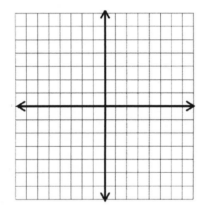

4) $x - 3y < -5$

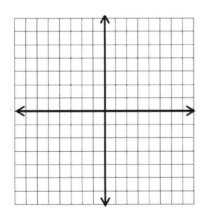

5) $6x - 2y \geq 8$

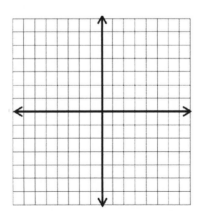

Finding Midpoint

Helpful	Midpoint of the segment AB:	Example:
Hints	$M\left(\dfrac{x_1+x_2}{2}, \dfrac{y_1+y_2}{2}\right)$	$(3, 9), (-1, 6)$ $M(1, 7.5)$

✎ **Find the midpoint of the line segment with the given endpoints.**

1) $(2, -2), (3, -5)$

2) $(0, 2), (-2, -6)$

3) $(7, 4), (9, -1)$

4) $(4, -5), (0, 8)$

5) $(1, -2), (1, -6)$

6) $(-2, -3), (3, -6)$

7) $(7, 0), (-7, 5)$

8) $(-2, 6), (-3, -2)$

9) $(-1, 1), (5, -5)$

10) $(2.3, -1.3), (-2.2, -0.5)$

11) $(4.1, 6.32), (4, 5.6)$

12) $(2, -1), (-6, 0)$

13) $(-4, 4), (5, -1)$

14) $(-2, -3), (-6, 5)$

15) $\left(\dfrac{1}{2}, 1\right), (2, 4)$

16) $(-2, -2), (6, 5)$

Finding Distance of Two Points

Helpful *Hints*	Distance from A to B: $$d = \sqrt{(x_1 - x_2)^2 + (y_1 - y_2)^2}$$	**Example:** $(-1, 2), (-1, -7)$ Distance = 9

✎*Find the distance between each pair of points.*

1) $(2, -1), (1, -1)$

2) $(6, 4), (-1, 3)$

3) $(-8, -5), (-6, 1)$

4) $(-6, -10), (-2, -10)$

5) $(4, -6), (-3, 4)$

6) $(-6, -7), (-2, -8)$

7) $(5, 4), (8, 2)$

8) $(8, 4), (3, -7)$

9) $(1, 3), (5, 7)$

10) $(4, 2), (-7, 1)$

11) $(-3, -4), (-7, -2)$

12) $(-7, -2), (6, 9)$

13) $(10, 0), (0, 4)$

14) $(-3, 2), (5, 0)$

15) $(-5, 6), (8, -4)$

16) $(3, -5), (-8, -4)$

17) $(0, 8), (4, 10)$

18) $(6, 4), (-5, -1)$

Answers of Worksheets – Chapter 8

Finding Slope

1) 2

2) $\dfrac{2}{7}$

3) −11

4) 0

5) $-\dfrac{1}{32}$

6) 1

7) $-\dfrac{3}{2}$

8) −1

9) $-\dfrac{1}{3}$

10) $\dfrac{11}{2}$

11) $-\dfrac{1}{17}$

12) $-\dfrac{22}{23}$

13) $-\dfrac{3}{4}$

14) $-\dfrac{5}{8}$

15) $-\dfrac{1}{14}$

16) $\dfrac{11}{20}$

17) Undefined

18) $-\dfrac{3}{19}$

Graphing Lines Using Slope–Intercept Form

1)

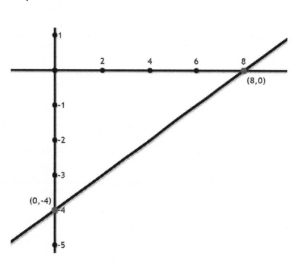

2)

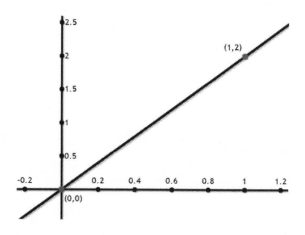

Graphing Lines Using Standard Form

1)

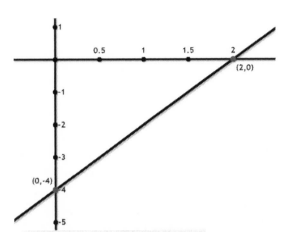

2)

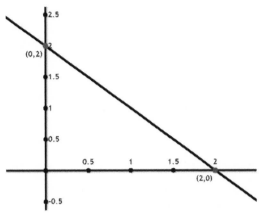

Writing Linear Equations

1) $y = 7x + 26$

2) $y = \frac{1}{9}x + \frac{31}{9}$

3) $y = -x - 2$

4) $y = -5x - 4$

5) $y = x + 3$

6) $y = -5x + 2$

7) $y = 2x - 5$

8) $y = 4$

9) $y = -2x + 1$

10) $y = 3x - 1$

11) $y = -x - 2$

12) $y = 4x - 9$

13) $y = 9x - 32$

14) $y = -2x + 3$

15) $y = \frac{8}{3}x - \frac{25}{3}$

16) $y = -\frac{3}{4}x - \frac{7}{2}$

17) $y = \frac{1}{4}x - \frac{5}{4}$

18) $y = -\frac{4}{3}x + \frac{19}{3}$

Graphing Linear Inequalities

1)

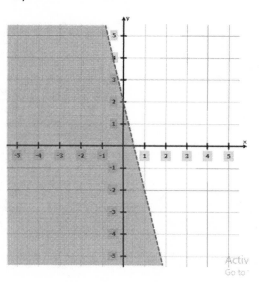

2)

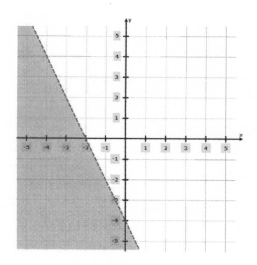

4)

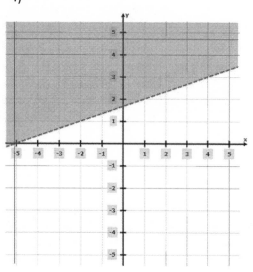

5)

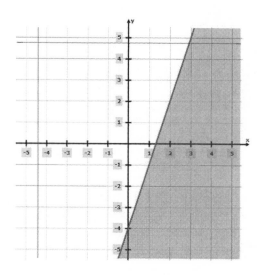

Finding Midpoint

1) (2.5, −3.5)

2) (−1, −2)

3) (8, 1.5)

4) (2, 1.5)

5) (1, −4)

6) (0.5, −4.5)

7) (0, 2.5)

8) (−2.5, 2)

9) (2, −2)

10) (0.05, −0.9)

11) (4.05, 5.96)

12) (−2, − 0.5)

13) $(\frac{1}{2}, 1\frac{1}{2})$

14) (−4, 1)

15) (1.25, 2.5)

16) $(2, \frac{3}{2})$

Finding Distance of Two Points

1) 1

2) 7.1

3) 6.32

4) 4

5) 12.21

6) 4.12

7) 3.61

8) 12.1

9) 5.66

10) 11.04

11) 4.47

12) 17.03

13) 10.77

14) 8.25

15) 16.4

16) 10.3

17) 4.47

18) 12.1

Chapter 9: Polynomials

Topics that you'll learn in this chapter:

- ✓ Classifying Polynomials
- ✓ Writing Polynomials in Standard Form
- ✓ Simplifying Polynomials
- ✓ Adding and Subtracting Polynomials
- ✓ Multiplying Monomials
- ✓ Multiplying and Dividing Monomials
- ✓ Multiplying a Polynomial and a Monomial
- ✓ Multiplying Binomials
- ✓ Factoring Trinomials
- ✓ Operations with Polynomials

Mathematics – the unshaken Foundation of Sciences, and the plentiful Fountain of Advantage to human

affairs. — Isaac Barrow

Classifying Polynomials

Helpful Hints

Name	Degree	Example
constant	0	4
linear	1	$2x$
quadratic	2	$x^2 + 5x + 6$
cubic	3	$x^3 - x^2 + 4x + 8$
quartic	4	$x^4 + 3x^3 - x^2 + 2x + 6$
quantic	5	$x^5 - 2x^4 + x^3 - x^2 + x + 10$

✍ *Name each polynomial by degree and number of terms.*

1) x

2) $-5x^4$

3) $7x - 4$

4) -6

5) $8x + 1$

6) $9x^2 - 8x^3$

7) $2x^5$

8) $10 + 8x$

9) $5x^2 - 6x$

10) $-7x^7 + 7x^4$

11) $-8x^4 + 5x^3 - 2x^2 - 8x$

12) $4x - 9x^2 + 4x^3 - 5x^4$

13) $4x^6 + 5x^5 + x^4$

14) $-4 - 2x^2 + 8x$

15) $9x^6 - 8$

16) $7x^5 + 10x^4 - 3x + 10x^7$

17) $4x^6 - 3x^2 - 8x^4$

18) $-5x^4 + 10x - 10$

Writing Polynomials in Standard Form

Helpful *Hints*	A polynomial function $f(x)$ of degree n is of the form $f(x) = a_n x^n + a_{n-1} x^{n-1} + \ldots + a_1 x + a_0$ The first term is the one with the biggest power!	**Example:** $2x^2 - 4x^3 - x =$ $-4x^3 + 2x^2 - x$

✎ **Write each polynomial in standard form.**

1) $3x^2 - 5x^3$

2) $3 + 4x^3 - 3$

3) $2x^2 + 1x - 6x^3$

4) $9x - 7x$

5) $12 - 7x + 9x^4$

6) $5x^2 + 13x - 2x^3$

7) $-3 + 16x - 16x$

8) $3x(x + 4) - 2(x + 4)$

9) $(x + 5)(x - 2)$

10) $3x^2 + x + 12 - 5x^2 - 2x$

11) $12x^5 + 7x^3 - 3x^5 - 8x^3$

12) $3x(2x + 5 - 2x^2)$

13) $11x(x^5 + 2x^3)$

14) $(x + 6)(x + 3)$

15) $(x + 4)^2$

16) $(8x - 7)(3x + 2)$

17) $5x(3x^2 + 2x + 1)$

18) $7x(3 - x + 6x^3)$

Simplifying Polynomials

Helpful	1– Find "like" terms. (they have same variables with same power).	**Example:**
Hints	2– Add or Subtract "like" terms using PEMDAS operation.	$2x^5 - 3x^3 + 8x^2 - 2x^5 =$ $- 3x^3 + 8x^2$

✎*Simplify each expression.*

1) $11 - 4x^2 + 3x^2 - 7x^3 + 3$

2) $2x^5 - x^3 + 8x^2 - 2x^5$

3) $(-5)(x^6 + 10) - 8(14 - x^6)$

4) $4(2x^2 + 4x^2 - 3x^3) + 6x^3 + 17$

5) $11 - 6x^2 + 5x^2 - 12x^3 + 22$

6) $2x^2 - 2x + 3x^3 + 12x - 22x$

7) $(3x - 8)(3x - 4)$

8) $(12x + 2y)^2$

9) $(12x^3 + 28x^2 + 10x + 4) \div (x + 2)$

10) $(2x + 12x^2 - 2) \div (2x + 1)$

11) $(2x^3 - 1) + (3x^3 - 2x^3)$

12) $(x - 5)(x - 3)$

13) $(3x + 8)(3x - 8)$

14) $(8x^2 - 3x) - (5x - 5 - 8x^2)$

Adding and Subtracting Polynomials

Helpful	Adding polynomials is just a matter of combining like terms, with some order of operations considerations thrown in.	**Example:**
Hints	Be careful with the minus signs, and don't confuse addition and multiplication!	$(3x^3 - 1) - (4x^3 + 2)$ $= -x^3 - 3$

✎ *Simplify each expression.*

1) $(2x^3 - 2) + (2x^3 + 2)$

2) $(4x^3 + 5) - (7 - 2x^3)$

3) $(4x^2 + 2x^3) - (2x^3 + 5)$

4) $(4x^2 - x) + (3x - 5x^2)$

5) $(7x + 9) - (3x + 9)$

6) $(4x^4 - 2x) - (6x - 2x^4)$

7) $(12x - 4x^3) - (8x^3 + 6x)$

8) $(2x^3 - 8x^2) - (5x^2 - 3x^3)$

9) $(2x^2 - 6) + (9x^2 - 4x^3)$

10) $(4x^3 + 3x^4) - (x^4 - 5x^3)$

11) $(-12x^4 + 10x^5 + 2x^3) + (14x^3 + 23x^5 + 8x^4)$

12) $(13x^2 - 6x^5 - 2x) - (-10x^2 - 11x^5 + 9x)$

13) $(35 + 9x^5 - 3x^2) + (8x^4 + 3x^5) - (27 - 5x^4)$

14) $(3x^5 - 2x^3 - 4x) + (4x + 10x^4 - 23) + (x^2 - x^3 + 12)$

Multiplying Monomials

Helpful	A monomial is a polynomial with just one term, like $2x$ or $7y$.	**Example:**
Hints		$2u^3 \times (-3u)$ $= -6u^4$

✎ *Simplify each expression.*

1) $2xy^2z \times 4z^2$

2) $4xy \times x^2y$

3) $4pq^3 \times (-2p^4q)$

4) $8s^4t^2 \times st^5$

5) $12p^3 \times (-3p^4)$

6) $-4p^2q^3r \times 6pq^2r^3$

7) $(-8a^4) \times (-12a^6b)$

8) $3u^4v^2 \times (-7u^2v^3)$

9) $4u^3 \times (-2u)$

10) $-6xy^2 \times 3x^2y$

11) $12y^2z^3 \times (-y^2z)$

12) $5a^2bc^2 \times 2abc^2$

Multiplying and Dividing Monomials

Helpful

Hints

- When you divide two monomials you need to divide their coefficients and then divide their variables.
- In case of exponents with the same base, you need to subtract their powers.

Example:

$(-3x^2)(8x^4y^{12}) = -24x^6y^{12}$

$\dfrac{36\,x^5y^7}{4\,x^4y^5} = 9xy^2$

✎ **Simplify.**

1) $(7x^4y^6)(4x^3y^4)$

2) $(15x^4)(3x^9)$

3) $(12x^2y^9)(7x^9y^{12})$

4) $\dfrac{80\;^{12}y^9}{10x^6y^7}$

5) $\dfrac{95x^{18}y^7}{5x^9y^2}$

6) $\dfrac{200x^3y^8}{40x^3y^7}$

7) $\dfrac{-15x^{17}y^{13}}{3x^6y^9}$

8) $\dfrac{-64x^8y^{10}}{8x^3y^7}$

Multiplying a Polynomial and a Monomial

Helpful	– When multiplying monomials, use the product rule for exponents.	**Example:**
Hints	– When multiplying a monomial by a polynomial, use the distributive property.	$2x(8x - 2) =$
	a × (b + c) = a × b + a × c	$16x^2 - 4x$

✎*Find each product.*

1) $5(3x - 6y)$

2) $9x(2x + 4y)$

3) $8x(7x - 4)$

4) $12x(3x + 9)$

5) $11x(2x - 11y)$

6) $2x(6x - 6y)$

7) $3x(2x^2 - 3x + 8)$

8) $13x(4x + 8y)$

9) $20(2x^2 - 8x - 5)$

10) $3x(3x - 2)$

11) $6x^3(3x^2 - 2x + 2)$

12) $8x^2(3x^2 - 5xy + 7y^2)$

13) $2x^2(3x^2 - 5x + 12)$

14) $2x^3(2x^2 + 5x - 4)$

15) $5x(6x^2 - 5xy + 2y^2)$

16) $9(x^2 + xy - 8y^2)$

Multiplying Binomials

Helpful	Use "FOIL". (First–Out–In–Last)	**Example:**
Hints	$(x + a)(x + b) = x^2 + (b + a)x + ab$	$(x + 2)(x - 3) =$ $x^2 - x - 6$

✎ **Multiply.**

1) $(3x - 2)(4x + 2)$

2) $(2x - 5)(x + 7)$

3) $(x + 2)(x + 8)$

4) $(x^2 + 2)(x^2 - 2)$

5) $(x - 2)(x + 4)$

6) $(x - 8)(2x + 8)$

7) $(5x - 4)(3x + 3)$

8) $(x - 7)(x - 6)$

9) $(6x + 9)(4x + 9)$

10) $(2x - 6)(5x + 6)$

11) $(x - 7)(x + 7)$

12) $(x + 4)(4x - 8)$

13) $(6x - 4)(6x + 4)$

14) $(x - 7)(x + 2)$

15) $(x - 8)(x + 8)$

16) $(3x + 3)(3x - 4)$

17) $(x + 3)(x + 3)$

18) $(x + 4)(x + 6)$

Factoring Trinomials

Helpful	"FOIL"	**Example:**
	$(x + a)(x + b) = x^2 + (b + a)x + ab$	$x^2 + 5x + 6 =$
Hints	"Difference of Squares"	$(x + 2)(x + 3)$
	$a^2 - b^2 = (a + b)(a - b)$	
	$a^2 + 2ab + b^2 = (a + b)(a + b)$	
	$a^2 - 2ab + b^2 = (a - b)(a - b)$	
	"Reverse FOIL"	
	$x^2 + (b + a)x + ab = (x + a)(x + b)$	

✎*Factor each trinomial.*

1) $x^2 - 7x + 12$

2) $x^2 + 5x - 14$

3) $x^2 - 11x - 42$

4) $6x^2 + x - 12$

5) $x^2 - 17x + 30$

6) $x^2 + 8x + 15$

7) $3x^2 + 11x - 4$

8) $x^2 - 6x - 27$

9) $10x^2 + 33x - 7$

10) $x^2 + 24x + 144$

11) $49x^2 + 28xy + 4y^2$

12) $16x^2 - 40x + 25$

13) $x^2 - 10x + 25$

14) $25x^2 - 20x + 4$

15) $x^3 + 6x^2y^2 + 9xy^3$

16) $9x^2 + 24x + 16$

17) $x^2 - 8x + 16$

18) $x^2 + 121 + 22x$

Operations with Polynomials

Helpful *Hints*	– When multiplying a monomial by a polynomial, use the distributive property. $a \times (b + c) = a \times b + a \times c$	**Example:** $5(6x - 1) =$ $30x - 5$

✎*Find each product.*

1) $3x^2 (6x - 5)$

2) $5x^2 (7x - 2)$

3) $-3 (8x - 3)$

4) $6x^3 (-3x + 4)$

5) $9 (6x + 2)$

6) $8 (3x + 7)$

7) $5 (6x - 1)$

8) $-7x^4 (2x - 4)$

9) $8 (x^2 + 2x - 3)$

10) $4 (4x^2 - 2x + 1)$

11) $2 (3x^2 + 2x - 2)$

12) $8x (5x^2 + 3x + 8)$

13) $(9x + 1)(3x - 1)$

14) $(4x + 5)(6x - 5)$

15) $(7x + 3)(5x - 6)$

16) $(3x - 4)(3x + 8)$

Answers of Worksheets – Chapter 9

Classifying Polynomials

1) Linear monomial
2) Quartic monomial
3) Linear binomial
4) Constant monomial
5) Linear binomial
6) Cubic binomial
7) Quantic monomial
8) Linear binomial
9) Quadratic binomial
10) Seventh degree binomial
11) Quartic polynomial with four terms
12) Quartic polynomial with four terms
13) Sixth degree trinomial
14) Quadratic trinomial
15) Sixth degree binomial
16) Seventh degree polynomial with four terms
17) Sixth degree trinomial
18) Quartic trinomial

Writing Polynomials in Standard Form

1) $-5x^3 + 3x^2$
2) $4x^3$
3) $-6x^3 + 2x^2 + x$
4) $2x$
5) $9x^4 - 7x + 12$
6) $-2x^3 + 5x^2 + 13x$
7) -3
8) $3x^2 + 10x - 8$
9) $x^2 + 3x - 10$
10) $-2x^2 - x + 12$
11) $9x^5 - x^3$
12) $-6x^3 + 6x^2 + 15x$
13) $11x^6 + 22x^4$
14) $x^2 + 9x + 18$
15) $x^2 + 8x + 16$
16) $24x^2 - 5x - 14$
17) $15x^3 + 10x^2 + 5x$
18) $42x^4 - 7x^2 + 21x$

Simplifying Polynomials

1) $-7x^3 - x^2 + 14$
2) $-x^3 + 8x^2$
3) $3x^6 - 162$
4) $-6x^3 + 24x^2 + 17$
5) $-12x^3 - x^2 + 33$
6) $3x^3 + 2x^2 - 12x$

7) $9x^2 - 36x + 32$

8) $144x^2 + 48xy + 4y^2$

9) $12x^2 + 4x + 2$

10) $6x - 1$

11) $3x^3 - 1$

12) $x^2 - 8x + 15$

13) $9x^2 - 64$

14) $16x^2 - 8x + 5$

Adding and Subtracting Polynomials

1) $4x^3$

2) $6x^3 - 2$

3) $4x^2 - 5$

4) $-x^2 + 2x$

5) $4x$

6) $6x^4 - 8x$

7) $-12x^3 + 6x$

8) $5x^3 - 13x^2$

9) $-4x^3 + 11x^2 - 6$

10) $2x^4 + 9x^3$

11) $33x^5 - 4x^4 + 16x^3$

12) $5x^5 + 23x^2 - 11x$

13) $12x^5 + 13x^4 - 3x^2 + 8$

14) $3x^5 + 10x^4 - 3x^3 + x^2 - 11$

Multiplying Monomials

1) $8xy^2z^3$

2) $4x^3y^2$

3) $-8p^5q^4$

4) $8s^5t^7$

5) $-36p^7$

6) $-24p^3q^5r^4$

7) $96a^{10}b$

8) $-21u^6v^5$

9) $-8u^4$

10) $-18x^3y^3$

11) $-12y^4z^4$

12) $10a^3b^2c^4$

Multiplying and Dividing Monomials

1) $28x^7y^{10}$

2) $45x^{13}$

3) $84x^{11}y^{21}$

4) $8x^6y^2$

5) $19x^9y^5$

6) $5y$

7) $-5x^{11}y^4$

8) $-8x^5y^3$

Multiplying a Polynomial and a Monomial

1) $15x - 30y$
2) $18x^2 + 36xy$
3) $56x^2 - 32x$
4) $36x^2 + 108x$
5) $22x^2 - 121xy$
6) $12x^2 - 12xy$
7) $6x^3 - 9x^2 + 24x$
8) $52x^2 + 104xy$

9) $40x^2 - 160x - 100$
10) $9x^2 - 6x$
11) $18x^5 - 12x^4 + 12x^3$
12) $24x^4 - 40x^3y + 56y^2x^2$
13) $6x^4 - 10x^3 + 24x^2$
14) $4x^5 + 10x^4 - 8x^3$
15) $30x^3 - 25x^2y + 10xy^2$
16) $9x^2 + 9xy - 72y^2$

Multiplying Binomials

1) $12x^2 - 2x - 4$
2) $2x^2 + 9x - 35$
3) $x^2 + 10x + 16$
4) $x^4 - 4$
5) $x^2 + 2x - 8$
6) $2x^2 - 8x - 64$
7) $15x^2 + 3x - 12$
8) $x^2 - 13x + 42$
9) $24x^2 + 90x + 81$

10) $10x^2 - 18x - 36$
11) $x^2 - 49$
12) $4x^2 + 8x - 32$
13) $36x^2 - 16$
14) $x^2 - 5x - 14$
15) $x^2 - 64$
16) $9x^2 - 3x - 12$
17) $x^2 + 6x + 9$
18) $x^2 + 10x + 24$

Factoring Trinomials

1) $(x - 3)(x - 4)$
2) $(x - 2)(x + 7)$
3) $(x + 3)(x - 14)$
4) $(2x + 3)(3x - 4)$
5) $(x - 15)(x - 2)$
6) $(x + 3)(x + 5)$
7) $(3x - 1)(x + 4)$
8) $(x - 9)(x + 3)$
9) $(5x - 1)(2x + 7)$

10) $(x + 12)(x + 12)$
11) $(7x + 2y)(7x + 2y)$
12) $(4x - 5)(4x - 5)$
13) $(x - 5)(x - 5)$
14) $(5x - 2)(5x - 2)$
15) $x(x^2 + 6xy^2 + 9y^3)$
16) $(3x + 4)(3x + 4)$
17) $(x - 4)(x - 4)$
18) $(x + 11)(x + 11)$

Operations with Polynomials

1) $18x^3 - 15x^2$

2) $35x^3 - 10x^2$

3) $-24x + 9$

4) $-18x^4 + 24x^3$

5) $54x + 18$

6) $24x + 56$

7) $30x - 5$

8) $-14x^5 + 28x^4$

9) $8x^2 + 16x - 24$

10) $16x^2 - 8x + 4$

11) $6x^2 + 4x - 4$

12) $40x^3 + 24x^2 + 64x$

13) $27x^2 - 6x - 1$

14) $24x^2 + 10x - 25$

15) $35x^2 - 27x - 18$

16) $9x^2 + 12x - 32$

Chapter 10: Quadratic and System of Equations

Topics that you'll learn in this chapter:

- ✓ Solve a Quadratic Equation

- ✓ Solving Systems of Equations by Substitution

- ✓ Solving Systems of Equations by Elimination

- ✓ Systems of Equations Word Problems

Mathematics is the door and key to the sciences. — Roger Bacon

Solve a Quadratic Equation

Helpful	Write the equation in the form of $ax^2 + bx + c = 0$ Factorize the quadratic. Use quadratic formula if you couldn't factorize the quadratic. **Quadratic formula** $$x = \frac{-b \pm \sqrt{b^2 - 4ac}}{2a}$$	**Example:** $x^2 + 5x + 6 = 0$ $(x + 3)(x + 2) = 0$ $(x + 3) = 0$ $x = -3$ $x + 2 = 0$ $x = -2$
Hints		

✎ *Solve each equation.*

1) $(x + 2)(x - 4) = 0$

2) $(x + 5)(x + 8) = 0$

3) $(3x + 2)(x + 3) = 0$

4) $(4x + 7)(2x + 5) = 0$

5) $x^2 - 11x + 19 = -5$
   +5   +5

   $x^2 - 11x + 24$

   $(x - 3)(x - 8)$ -3⧸-8
                        -11
   $x = 3$ $x = 8$

6) $x^2 + 7x + 18 = 8$
   -8 = 8

   $x = -5$ $x = -2$ -10
                      5⧸2
                        7

7) $x^2 - 10x + 22 = -2$ 24
   +2   +2   -6⧸-4
                          -10
   $x = 6$ $x = 4$

8) $x^2 + 3x - 12 = 6$
   = 6 -6

   $x - 3$
   $x = 6$ $x = 3$ -14⧸-8
                          3

9) $18x^2 + 45x - 27 = 0$

10) $90x^2 - 84x = -18$

Solving Systems of Equations by Substitution

Helpful Hints	Consider the system of equations $x - y = 1, -2x + y = 6$ Substitute x = 1 − y in the second equation $-2(1 - y) + y = 5 \qquad y = 2$ Substitute $y = 2$ in $x = 1 + y$ $x = 1 + 2 = 3$	**Example:** $- 2x - 2y = -13$ $- 4x + 2y = 10$ $(0.5, 6)$

✎ *Solve each system of equation by substitution.*

1) $- 2x + 2y = 4$ $-2x + 2y = 4$
$- 2x + y = 3$ $+4x + 2y = -6$

$-2(-1) + y = 3$ $\frac{2y}{2} = \frac{-2}{2}$
$+2 + y = 3 \quad y = 1$ $x = -1$

2) $- 10x + 2y = - 6$

$6x - 16y = 48$

3) $y = - 8$

$16x - 12y = 72$

4) $2y = - 6x + 10$

$10x - 8y = - 6$
$-10x \qquad -10x$

$-8y = -10x - 6$
$4 \, 2y = -6x + 10$
$8y = -24x + 40$

$\frac{-34x + 34}{34} \quad x=1$

$2y = -6(1) + 10$
$2y = -6 + 10$
$\frac{2y}{2} = \frac{4}{2}$
$y = 2$

5) $3x - 9y = - 3$

$3y = 3x - 3$

6) $- 4x + 12y = 12$

$- 14x + 16y = - 10$

7) $x + 20y = 20$

$- x + 15y = 5$
$+x - 15y = -5$
$\frac{5y}{5} = \frac{15}{5} \quad y = 3$

$x + 20(3) = 20$
$x + 60 = 20$
$\quad -60 \quad -60$
$x = 40$

8) $2x + 8y = 28$

$- 2x - 2y = 5$
$-2x + 4y = -10$
$2x + 6y = 28$

$\frac{12y}{12} = \frac{18}{12}$
$y = \frac{3}{2}$

$x - 2(\frac{3}{2}) = 5$
$x - 3 = 5$
$\quad +3 \quad +3$
$x = 8$

Solving Systems of Equations by Elimination

Helpful	-	The elimination method for solving systems of linear equations uses the addition property of equality. You can add the same value to each side of an equation.	**Example:** $x + 2y = 6$ $+ -x + y = 3$ $\overline{ 3y = 9}$ $y = 3$ $x + 6 = 6$ $x = 0$
Hints			

✎ *Solve each system of equation by elimination.*

1) $10x - 9y = -12$

   $-5x + 3y = 6$

5) $32x + 14y = 52$

   $16x - 4y = -40$

2) $-3x - 4y = 5$

   $x - 2y = 5$

6) $2x - 8y = -6$

   $8x + 2y = 10$

3) $5x - 14y = 22$

   $-6x + 7y = 3$

7) $-4x + 4y = -4$

   $4x + 2y = 10$

4) $10x - 14y = -4$

   $-10x - 20y = -30$

8) $4x + 6y = 10$

   $8x + 12y = -20$

Systems of Equations Word Problems

Helpful *Hints*	Define your variables, Write two equations, and use one of the methods for solving systems of equations to solve.

Example:

The difference of two numbers is 6. Their sum is 14. Find the numbers.

$x + y = 6$

$x + y = 14$ (10, 4)

✎ Solve.

1) A farmhouse shelters 10 animals, some are pigs and some are ducks. Altogether there are 36 legs. How many of each animal are there?

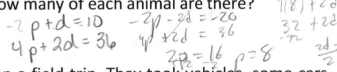

$p + d = 10$

$p| + d| = 36$

2) A class of 195 students went on a field trip. They took vehicles, some cars and some buses. Find the number of cars and the number of buses they took if each car holds 5 students and each bus hold 45 students.

3) The difference of two numbers is 6. Their sum is 14. Find the numbers.

$x + y = 14$ $x = 10$ $x + y = 14$

$2x + y = 6$ $y = 4$ $x - y = 6$

4) The sum of the digits of a certain two–digit number is 7. Reversing its increasing the number by 9. What is the number?

5) The difference of two numbers is 18. Their sum is 66. Find the numbers.

$x + y = 66$

$x + y = 18$

$42 - y = 18$

$-42 \quad -42$

$-y = 24$

$y = -24$

$x = 42$

$y = 24$

Answers of Worksheets – Chapter 10

Solving Quadratic Equations

1) $x = -2, x = 4$

2) $x = -5, x = -8$

3) $x = -\frac{2}{3}, x = -3$

4) $x = -\frac{7}{4}, x = -\frac{5}{2}$

5) $x = 8, x = 3$

6) $x = -5, x = -2$

7) $x = 6, x = 4$

8) $x = -6, x = 3$

9) $x = \frac{1}{2}, x = -3$

10) $x = \frac{3}{5}, x = \frac{1}{3}$

Solving Systems of Equations by Substitution

1) $(-1, 1)$

2) $(0, -3)$

3) $(-4, -8)$

4) $(1, 2)$

5) $(2, 1)$

6) $(3, 2)$

7) $(-4, 3)$

8) $(8, \frac{3}{2})$

Solving Systems of Equations by Elimination

1) $(-1.2, 0)$

2) $(1, -2)$

3) $(-4, -3)$

4) $(1, 1)$

5) $(-1, 6)$

6) $(1, 1)$

7) $(2, 1)$

8) No solution

Systems of Equations Word Problems

1) There are 8 pigs and 2 ducks.

2) There are 3 cars and 4 buses.

3) 10 and 4.

4) 34

5) 24 and 42

Chapter 11: Quadratic Functions

Topics that you'll learn in this chapter:

✓ Graphing Quadratic Functions

✓ Solving Quadratic Equations

✓ Use the Quadratic Formula and the Discriminant

✓ Solve Quadratic Inequalities

It's fine to work on any problem, so long as it generates interesting mathematics along the way – even if

you don't solve it at the end of the day." – Andrew Wiles

Graphing Quadratic Functions

Quadratic functions in vertex form: $y = a(x - h)^2 + k$, vertex: (h, k)

Quadratic functions in standard form: $y = ax^2 + bx + c$, vertex: (h, k), $h = \frac{-b}{2a}$

$$k = ah^2 + bh + c$$

- Step 1: Find the vertex of the quadratic function.
- Step 2: Plug in some values of x and solve for y. Then, find the points and graph the function.

✎ **Sketch the graph of each function. Identify the vertex and axis of symmetry.**

1) $y = 3(x + 1)^2 + 2$

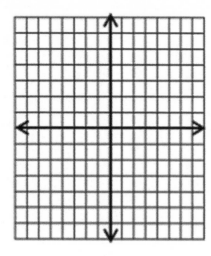

2) $y = -(x - 2)^2 - 4$

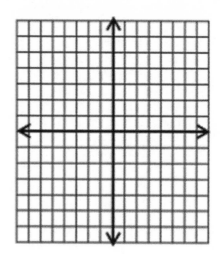

3) $y = 2(x - 3)^2 + 8$

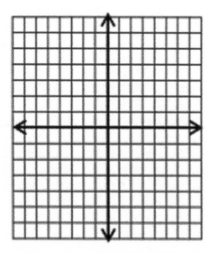

4) $y = x^2 - 8x + 19$

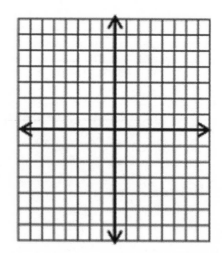

Solving Quadratic Equations

Helpful *Hints*	Write the equation in the form of $ax^2 + bx + c = 0$ Factorize the quadratic. Use quadratic formula if you couldn't factorize the quadratic. **Quadratic formula** $$x = \frac{-b \pm \sqrt{b^2 - 4ac}}{2a}$$

✍ *Solve each equation by factoring or by using the quadratic formula.*

1) $x^2 + x - 20 = 2x$

2) $x^2 + 8x = -15$

3) $7x^2 - 14x = -7$

4) $6x^2 - 18x - 18 = 6$

5) $2x^2 + 6x - 24 = 12$

6) $2x^2 - 22x + 38 = -10$

7) $(2x + 5)(4x + 3) = 0$

8) $(x + 2)(x - 7) = 0$

9) $(x + 3)(x + 5) = 0$

10) $(5x + 7)(x + 4) = 0$

11) $-4x^2 - 8x - 3 = -3 - 5x^2$

12) $10x^2 = 27x - 18$

13) $7x^2 - 6x + 3 = 3$

14) $x^2 = 2x$

15) $2x^2 - 14 = -3x$

16) $10x^2 - 26x = -12$

17) $15x^2 + 80 = -80x$

18) $x^2 + 15x = -56$

Use the Quadratic Formula and the Discriminant

Helpful	- Discriminant determines the number of solutions for the given quadratic equation.
	- The discriminant, is the part of the quadratic formula under the square root.
Hints	$x = \dfrac{-b \pm \sqrt{b^2 - 4ac}}{2a}$
	- If discriminant is positive, there are 2 solutions, if it's zero, there is one solution, and if it's negative, there is no solution for the quadratic function.

✎ **Find the value of the discriminant of each quadratic equation.**

1) $2x^2 + 5x - 4 = 0$

2) $x^2 + 5x + 2 = 0$

3) $5x^2 + x - 2 = 0$

4) $-4x^2 - 4x + 5 = 0$

5) $-2x^2 - x - 1 = 0$

6) $6x^2 - 2x - 3 = 0$

7) $x\,(x - 1)$

8) $8x^2 - 9x = 0$

9) $3x^2 - 5x + 1 = 0$

10) $5x^2 + 6x + 4 = 0$

✎ **Find the discriminant of each quadratic equation then state the number of real and imaginary solution.**

11) $8x^2 - 6x + 3 = 5x^2$

12) $-4x^2 - 4x = 6$

13) $-x^2 - 9 = 6x$

14) $-9x^2 = -8x + 8$

15) $4x^2 = 8x - 4$

16) $9x^2 + 6x + 6 = 5$

17) $9x^2 - 3x - 8 = -10$

18) $-2x^2 - 8x - 14 = -6$

Solve Quadratic Inequalities

Helpful	- A quadratic inequality is one that can be written in one of the following standard forms: $$ax^2 + bx + c > 0$$ $$ax^2 + bx + c < 0$$ $$ax^2 + bx + c \geq 0$$ $$ax^2 + bx + c \leq 0$$
Hints	- Solving quadratic inequality is similar to quadratic equations. - In inequalities, we need to find a range of values of x that work in the inequality. - Step 1: Solve the inequality and find the factors. (find the zeros) - Step 2: Choose testing points to test each interval. - Step 3: Determine the sign of the overall quadratic function in each interval.

✎ *Solve each quadratic inequality.*

1) $-x^2 - 5x + 6 > 0$

2) $x^2 - 5x - 6 < 0$

3) $x^2 + 4x - 5 > 0$

4) $x^2 - 2x - 3 \geq 0$

5) $x^2 - 1 < 0$

6) $17x^2 + 15x - 2 \geq 0$

7) $4x^2 + 20x - 11 < 0$

8) $12x^2 + 10x - 12 > 0$

9) $18x^2 + 23x + 5 \leq 0$

10) $-9x^2 + 29x - 6 \geq 0$

11) $-8x^2 + 6x - 1 \leq 0$

12) $5x^2 - 15x + 10 < 0$

13) $3x^2 - 5x \geq 4x^2 + 6$

14) $x^2 > 5x + 6$

15) $3x^2 + 7x \leq 5x^2 + 3x - 6$

16) $4x^2 - 12 > 3x^2 + x$

17) $3x^2 - 5x \geq 4x^2 + 6$

18) $2x^2 + 2x - 8 > x^2$

Answers of Worksheets – Chapter 11

Graphing quadratic functions

1)

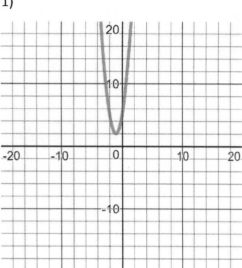

2)

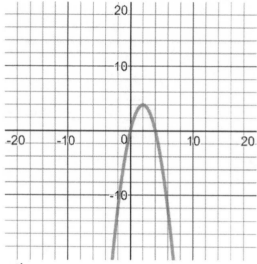

3)

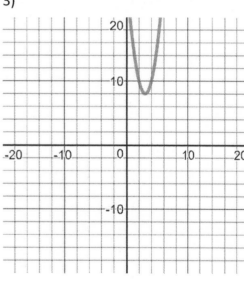

4)

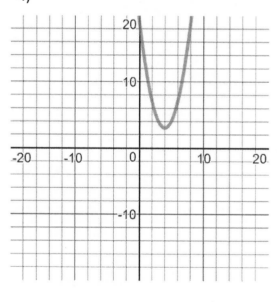

Solving quadratic equations

1) $\{5, -4\}$

2) $\{-5, -3\}$

3) $\{1\}$

4) $\{4, -1\}$

5) $\{3, -6\}$

6) $\{3, 8\}$

7) $\{-\frac{5}{2}, -\frac{3}{4}\}$

8) $\{-2, 7\}$

9) $\{-3, -5\}$

10) $\{-\frac{7}{5}, -4\}$

11) $\{8, 0\}$

12) $\{\frac{6}{5}, \frac{3}{2}\}$

13) $\{\frac{6}{7}, 0\}$

14) $\{2, 0\}$

15) $\{-\frac{7}{2}, 2\}$

16) $\{\frac{3}{5}, 2\}$

17) $\{-\frac{4}{3}, -4\}$

18) $\{-8, -7\}$

Use the quadratic formula and the discriminant

1) 57

2) 17

3) 41

4) 96

5) −7

6) 76

7) 21

8) 81

9) 13

10) −44

11) 0, one real solution

12) −80, no solution

13) 0, one real solution

14) −224, no solution

15) 0, one real solution

16) 0, one real solution

17) −63, solution

18) 0, one real solution

Solve quadratic inequalities

1) $-6 < x < 1$

2) $-1 < x < 6$

3) $x < -5$ or $x > 1$

4) $x \leq -1$ or $x \geq 3$

5) $-1 < x < 1$

6) $x \leq -1$ or $x \geq \frac{2}{17}$

7) $-\frac{11}{2} < x < \frac{1}{2}$

8) $x < -\frac{3}{2}$ or $x > \frac{2}{3}$

9) $-1 \leq x \leq -\frac{5}{18}$

10) $\frac{2}{9} \leq x \leq 3$

11) $x \leq \frac{1}{4}$ or $x \geq \frac{1}{2}$

12) $1 < x < 2$

13) $-3 \leq x \leq -2$

14) $x < -1$ or $x > 6$

15) $x \leq -1$ or $x \geq 3$

16) $x < -3$ or $x > 4$

17) $-3 \leq x \leq -2$

18) $x < -4$ or $x > 2$

Chapter 12: Complex numbers

Topics that you'll learn in this chapter:

- ✓ Adding and Subtracting Complex Numbers

- ✓ Multiplying and Dividing Complex Numbers

- ✓ Graphing Complex Numbers

- ✓ Rationalizing Imaginary Denominators

Mathematics is a hard thing to love. It has the unfortunate habit, like a rude dog, of turning its most unfavorable side towards you when you first make contact with it. — David Whiteland

Adding and Subtracting Complex Numbers

Helpful	**Adding:**	**Example:**
	$(a + bi) + (c + di) = (a + c) + (b + d)i$	$-5 + (2 - 4i) = -3 - 4i$
Hints	**Subtracting:**	$(2 - 5i) + (4 - 6i) =$
	$(a + bi) - (c + di) = (a - c) + (b - d)i$	$6 - 11i$

✎ *Simplify.*

1) $-8 + (2i) + (-8 + 6i)$

2) $12 - (5i) + (4 - 14i)$

3) $-2 + (-8 - 7i) - 9$

4) $(-18 - 3i) + (11 + 5i)$

5) $(3 + 5i) + (8 + 3i)$

6) $(8 - 3i) + (4 + i)$

7) $3 + (2 - 4i)$

8) $(10 + 9i) + (6 + 8i)$

9) $(-5i) - (-5 + 2i)$

10) $(-14 + i) - (-12 - 11i)$

11) $(-12i) + (2 - 6i) + 10$

12) $(-11 - 9i) - (-9 - 3i)$

13) $(13i) - (17 + 3i)$

14) $(-3 + 6i) - (-9 - i)$

15) $(-5 + 15i) - (-3 + 3i)$

16) $(-12i) + (2 - 6i) + 10$

Multiplying and Dividing Complex Numbers

Helpful Hints

Multiplying:

$$(a + bi) + (c + di) = (ac - bd) + (ad + bc)i$$

Dividing:

$$\frac{a+bi}{c+di} = \frac{a+bi}{c+di} \cdot \frac{c-di}{c-di} = \frac{ac+b}{c^2+d^2} + \frac{bc+a}{c^2+d^2}i$$

✎**Simplify.**

1) $(4i)(-i)(2-5i)$

2) $(2-8i)(3-5i)$

3) $(-5+9i)(3+5i)$

4) $(7+3i)(7+8i)$

5) $(5+4i)^2$

6) $2(3i) - (5i)(-8+5i)$

7) $\dfrac{2+4i}{14+4i}$

8) $\dfrac{4-3i}{-4i}$

9) $\dfrac{5+6i}{-1+8i}$

10) $\dfrac{-8-i}{-4-6i}$

11) $\dfrac{5+9i}{i}$

12) $\dfrac{12}{-9+3i}$

13) $\dfrac{5}{-10i}$

14) $\dfrac{-3-10}{5i}$

15) $\dfrac{9i}{3-i}$

16) $\dfrac{-1+5i}{-8-7i}$

17) $\dfrac{-2-9i}{-2+7i}$

18) $\dfrac{4+i}{2-5i}$

Graphing Complex Numbers

Helpful	- Complex numbers can be plotted on the complex coordinate plane.
	- The horizontal line is Real axis and the vertical line is Imaginary axis.
Hints	- Complex numbers are written in the form of: $A + Bi$, where A is real number and B is number of units up or down.
	For example: The point 3 + 4i, is located 3 units to the right of origin and 4 units up.

✎ *Identify each complex number graphed.*

1)

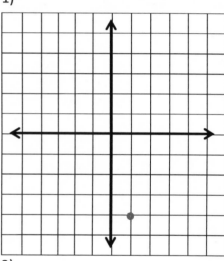

2)

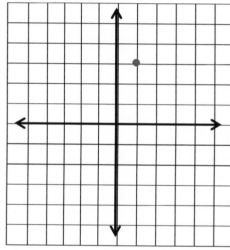

3)

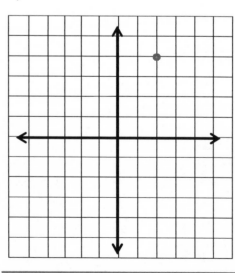

4)

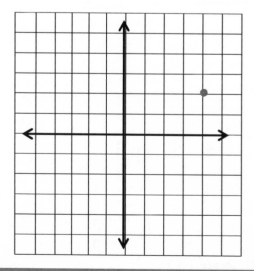

Rationalizing Imaginary Denominators

Helpful *Hints*	Step 1: Find the conjugate (it's the denominator with different sign between the two terms.
	Step 2: Multiply numerator and denominator by the conjugate.
	Step 3: Simplify if needed.
	Example: $\dfrac{5i}{2-3i} = \dfrac{5i(2+3i)}{(2-3i)(2+3i)} = \dfrac{10i+1}{4-9i^2}^{\,2} = \dfrac{-15+1}{13}$

✎ *Simplify.*

1) $\dfrac{10-10i}{-5i}$

2) $\dfrac{4-9i}{-6i}$

3) $\dfrac{6+8i}{9i}$

4) $\dfrac{8i}{-1+3i}$

5) $\dfrac{5i}{-2-6i}$

6) $\dfrac{-10-5i}{-6+6i}$

7) $\dfrac{-5-9i}{9+8i}$

8) $\dfrac{-5-3i}{7-10i}$

9) $\dfrac{-1+i}{-5i}$

10) $\dfrac{-6-i}{i}$

11) $\dfrac{a}{ib}$

12) $\dfrac{-4-i}{9+5i}$

13) $\dfrac{-3+i}{-2i}$

14) $\dfrac{-5}{-i}$

15) $\dfrac{-6-i}{-1+6i}$

16) $\dfrac{-9-3i}{-3+3i}$

17) $\dfrac{6}{-4i}$

18) $\dfrac{8i}{-1+3i}$

Answers of Worksheets – Chapter 12

Adding and Subtracting Complex Numbers

1) $-16 + 8i$

2) $16 - 19i$

3) $-19 - 7i$

4) $-7 + 2i$

5) $11 + 8i$

6) $12 - 2i$

7) $5 - 4i$

8) $16 + 17i$

9) $5 - 7i$

10) $-2 + 12i$

11) $12 - 18i$

12) $-2 - 6i$

13) $-17 + 10i$

14) $6 + 7i$

15) $-2 + 12i$

16) $12 - 18i$

Multiplying and Dividing Complex Numbers

1) $8 - 20i$

2) $-34 - 34i$

3) $-60 + 2i$

4) $25 + 77i$

5) $9 + 40i$

6) $25 + 46i$

7) $\frac{11+12}{53}$

8) $\frac{3}{4} + i$

9) $\frac{19}{26} - \frac{11}{13}i$

10) $\frac{2-6i}{5}$

11) $-5i + 9$

12) $\frac{-3i+1}{6}$

13) $\frac{i}{2}$

14) $\frac{3i-10}{5}$

15) $\frac{27i-9}{10}$

16) $-\frac{27}{113} - \frac{47}{113}$

17) $-\frac{59}{53} + \frac{32i}{53}$

18) $\frac{3}{29} + \frac{22i}{29}$

Graphing Complex Numbers

1) $1 - 4i$

2) $1 + 3i$

3) $2 + 4i$

4) $4 + 2i$

Rationalizing Imaginary Denominators

1) $2i + 2$

2) $\dfrac{4 + 9i}{6}$

3) $\dfrac{6+8i}{9}$

4) $\dfrac{-4i+1}{5}$

5) $\dfrac{-i-3}{4}$

6) $\dfrac{5+15i}{12}$

7) $\dfrac{-117-41i}{145}$

8) $\dfrac{-5-71}{149}$

9) $\dfrac{-i-1}{5}$

10) $6i - 1$

11) $-\dfrac{ia}{b}$

12) $\dfrac{-41+1}{106}$

13) $\dfrac{-1-3i}{2}$

14) $-5i$

15) $0 + 1i$

16) $-3 + 3i$

17) $\dfrac{3i}{2}$

18) $\dfrac{-4i+12}{5}$

Chapter 13: Exponents and Radicals

Topics that you'll learn in this chapter:

- ✓ Multiplication Property of Exponents
- ✓ Division Property of Exponents
- ✓ Powers of Products and Quotients
- ✓ Zero and Negative Exponents
- ✓ Negative Exponents and Negative Bases
- ✓ Writing Scientific Notation
- ✓ Square Roots

Mathematics is no more computation than typing is literature.

– John Allen Paulos

Multiplication Property of Exponents

Helpful Hints

Exponents rules

$x^a \cdot x^b = x^{a+b}$ $x^a / x^b = x^{a-b}$

$1/x^b = x^{-b}$ $(x^a)^b = x^{a \cdot b}$

$(xy)^a = x^a \cdot y^a$

Example:

$(x^2y)^3 = x^6y^3$

✎ **Simplify.**

1) $4^2 \cdot 4^2$

2) $2 \cdot 2^2 \cdot 2^2$

3) $3^2 \cdot 3^2$

4) $3x^3 \cdot x$

5) $12x^4 \cdot 3x$

6) $6x \cdot 2x^2$

7) $5x^4 \cdot 5x^4$

8) $6x^2 \cdot 6x^3y^4$

9) $7x^2y^5 \cdot 9xy^3$

10) $7xy^4 \cdot 4x^3y^3$

11) $(2x^2)^2$

12) $3x^5y^3 \cdot 8x^2y^3$

13) $7x^3 \cdot 10y^3x^5 \cdot 8yx^3$

14) $(x^4)^3$

15) $(2x^2)^4$

16) $(x^2)^3$

17) $(6x)^2$

18) $3x^4y^5 \cdot 7x^2y^3$

Division Property of Exponents

Helpful	$\frac{x^a}{x^b} = x^{a-b}$, $x \neq 0$	**Example:**
Hints		$\frac{x^{12}}{x^5} = x^7$

✎ *Simplify.*

1) $\dfrac{5^5}{5}$

2) $\dfrac{3}{3^5}$

3) $\dfrac{2^2}{2^3}$

4) $\dfrac{2^4}{2^2}$

5) $\dfrac{x}{x^3}$

6) $\dfrac{3x^3}{9x^4}$

7) $\dfrac{2x^{-5}}{9x^{-2}}$

8) $\dfrac{21^8}{7x^3}$

9) $\dfrac{7x^6}{4x^7}$

10) $\dfrac{6x^2}{4x^3}$

11) $\dfrac{5x}{10^3}$

12) $\dfrac{3x^3}{2x^5}$

13) $\dfrac{12^3}{14^6}$

14) $\dfrac{12^3}{9y^8}$

15) $\dfrac{25xy^4}{5x^6y^2}$

16) $\dfrac{2x^4}{7x}$

17) $\dfrac{16x^2y^8}{4x^3}$

18) $\dfrac{12x^4}{15x^7y^9}$

19) $\dfrac{12y^4}{10yx^8}$

20) $\dfrac{16x^4y}{9x^8y^2}$

21) $\dfrac{5x^8}{20^8}$

Powers of Products and Quotients

Helpful	For any nonzero numbers a and b and any integer x, (ab)^x = a^x . b^x.	**Example:**
Hints		$(2x^2 . y^3)^2 =$ $4x^2 . y^6$

✎ *Simplify.*

1) $(2x^3)^4$

2) $(4xy^4)^2$

3) $(5x^4)^2$

4) $(11x^5)^2$

5) $(4x^2y^4)^4$

6) $(2x^4y^4)^3$

7) $(3x^2y^2)^2$

8) $(3x^4y^3)^4$

9) $(2x^6y^8)^2$

10) $(12x \ 3x)^3$

11) $(2x^9 \ x^6)^3$

12) $(5x^{10}y^3)^3$

13) $(4x^3 \ x^2)^2$

14) $(3x^3 \ 5x)^2$

15) $(10x^{11}y^3)^2$

16) $(9x^7 \ y^{\,5})^2$

17) $(4x^4y^6)^5$

18) $(4x^4)^2$

19) $(3x \ 4y^3)^2$

20) $(9x^2y)^3$

21) $(12x^2y^5)^2$

Zero and Negative Exponents

Helpful *Hints*	A negative exponent simply means that the base is on the wrong side of the fraction line, so you need to flip the base to the other side. For instance, "x^{-2}" (pronounced as "ecks to the minus two") just means "x^2" but underneath, as in $\frac{1}{x^2}$	**Example:** $5^{-2} = \frac{1}{25}$

✎ *Evaluate the following expressions.*

1) 8^{-2}

2) 2^{-4}

3) 10^{-2}

4) 5^{-3}

5) 22^{-1}

6) 9^{-1}

7) 3^{-2}

8) 4^{-2}

9) 5^{-2}

10) 35^{-1}

11) 6^{-3}

12) 0^{15}

13) 10^{-9}

14) 3^{-4}

15) 5^{-2}

16) 2^{-3}

17) 3^{-3}

18) 8^{-1}

19) 7^{-3}

20) 6^{-2}

21) $(\frac{2}{3})^{-2}$

22) $(\frac{1}{5})^{-3}$

23) $(\frac{1}{2})^{-8}$

24) $(\frac{2}{5})^{-3}$

25) 10^{-3}

26) 1^{-10}

Negative Exponents and Negative Bases

Helpful	– Make the power positive. A negative exponent is the reciprocal of that number with a positive exponent.	**Example:**
Hints	– The parenthesis is important!	$2x^{-3} = \dfrac{2}{x^3}$

$- 5^{-2}$ is not the same as $(- 5)^{-2}$

$- 5^{-2} = -\dfrac{1}{5^2}$ and $(- 5)^{-2} = +\dfrac{1}{5^2}$

✎ *Simplify.*

1) $- 6^{-1}$

2) $- 4x^{-3}$

3) $-\dfrac{5x}{x^{-3}}$

4) $-\dfrac{a^{-3}}{b^{-2}}$

5) $-\dfrac{5}{x^{-3}}$

6) $\dfrac{7b}{-9c^{-4}}$

7) $-\dfrac{5n^{-2}}{10^{\ -3}}$

8) $\dfrac{4a^{\ -2}}{-3c^{-2}}$

9) $- 12x^2y^{-3}$

10) $\left(-\dfrac{1}{3}\right)^{-2}$

11) $\left(-\dfrac{3}{4}\right)^{-2}$

12) $\left(\dfrac{3a}{2c}\right)^{-2}$

13) $\left(-\dfrac{5x}{3yz}\right)^{-3}$

14) $-\dfrac{2x}{a^{-4}}$

Writing Scientific Notation

Helpful

Hints

– It is used to write very big or very small numbers in decimal form.

– In scientific notation all numbers are written in the form of:

$$m \times 10^n$$

Decimal notation	Scientific notation
5	5×10^0
−25,000	-2.5×10^4
0.5	5×10^{-1}
2,122.456	$2,122456 \times 10^3$

✎ *Write each number in scientific notation.*

1) 91×10^3

2) 60

3) 2000000

4) 0.0000006

5) 354000

6) 0.000325

7) 2.5

8) 0.00023

9) 56000000

10) 2000000

11) 78000000

12) 0.0000022

13) 0.00012

14) 0.004

15) 78

16) 1600

17) 1450

18) 130000

19) 60

20) 0.113

21) 0.02

Square Roots

Helpful	— A square root of x is a number r whose square is: $r^2 = x$	**Example:**
Hints	r is a square root of x.	$\sqrt{4} = 2$

✎ *Find the value each square root.*

1) $\sqrt{1}$

2) $\sqrt{4}$

3) $\sqrt{9}$

4) $\sqrt{25}$

5) $\sqrt{16}$

6) $\sqrt{49}$

7) $\sqrt{36}$

8) $\sqrt{0}$

9) $\sqrt{64}$

10) $\sqrt{81}$

11) $\sqrt{121}$

12) $\sqrt{225}$

13) $\sqrt{144}$

14) $\sqrt{100}$

15) $\sqrt{256}$

16) $\sqrt{289}$

17) $\sqrt{324}$

18) $\sqrt{400}$

19) $\sqrt{900}$

20) $\sqrt{529}$

21) $\sqrt{90}$

Answers of Worksheets – Chapter 13

Multiplication Property of Exponents

1) 4^4
2) 2^5
3) 3^4
4) $3x^4$
5) $36x^5$
6) $12x^3$

7) $25x^8$
8) $36x^5y^4$
9) $63x^3y^8$
10) $28x^4y^7$
11) $4x^4$
12) $24x^7y^6$

13) $560x^{11}y^4$
14) x^{12}
15) $16x^8$
16) x^6
17) $36x^2$
18) $21x^6y^8$

Division Property of Exponents

1) 5^4
2) $\frac{1}{3^4}$
3) $\frac{1}{2}$
4) 2^2
5) $\frac{1}{x^2}$
6) $\frac{1}{3x}$
7) $\frac{2}{9x^3}$
8) $3x^5$

9) $\frac{7}{4x}$
10) $\frac{3}{2x}$
11) $\frac{1}{2x^2}$
12) $\frac{3}{2x^2}$
13) $\frac{6}{7x^3}$
14) $\frac{4x^3}{3y^8}$
15) $\frac{5y^2}{x^5}$

16) $\frac{2x^3}{7}$
17) $\frac{4y^8}{x}$
18) $\frac{4}{5x^3y^9}$
19) $\frac{6}{5x^4}$
20) $\frac{16}{9x^4y}$
21) $\frac{1}{4}$

Powers of Products and Quotients

1) $16x^{12}$
2) $16x^2y^8$
3) $25x^8$
4) $121x^{10}$
5) $256x^8y^{16}$
6) $8x^{12}y^{12}$

7) $9x^4y^4$
8) $81x^{16}y^{12}$
9) $4x^{12}y^{16}$
10) $46,656x^6$
11) $8x^{45}$
12) $125x^{30}y^9$

13) $16x^{10}$
14) $225x^8$
15) $100x^{22}y^6$
16) $81x^{14}y^{10}$
17) $1,024x^{20}y^{30}$
18) $16x^8$

19) $144x^2y^6$ 20) $729x^6y^3$ 21) $144x^4y^{10}$

Zero and Negative Exponents

1) $\frac{1}{64}$ 9) $\frac{1}{25}$ 17) $\frac{1}{27}$

2) $\frac{1}{16}$ 10) $\frac{1}{35}$ 18) $\frac{1}{8}$

3) $\frac{1}{100}$ 11) $\frac{1}{216}$ 19) $\frac{1}{343}$

4) $\frac{1}{125}$ 12) 0 20) $\frac{1}{36}$

5) $\frac{1}{22}$ 13) $\frac{1}{1000000000}$ 21) $\frac{9}{4}$

6) $\frac{1}{9}$ 14) $\frac{1}{81}$ 22) 125

7) $\frac{1}{9}$ 15) $\frac{1}{25}$ 23) 256

8) $\frac{1}{16}$ 16) $\frac{1}{8}$ 24) $\frac{125}{8}$

Negative Exponents and Negative Bases

1) $-\frac{1}{6}$ 6) $-\frac{7bc^4}{9}$ 10) 9

2) $-\frac{4}{x^3}$ 7) $-\frac{p^3}{2n^2}$ 11) $\frac{16}{9}$

3) $-5x^4$ 8) $-\frac{4ac^2}{3b^2}$ 12) $\frac{4c^2}{9a^2}$

4) $-\frac{b^2}{a^3}$ 9) $-\frac{12^2}{y^3}$ 13) $-\frac{27y^3z^3}{125x^3}$

5) $-5x^3$ 14) $-2xa^4$

Writing Scientific Notation

1) 9.1×10^4 6) 3.25×10^{-4} 11) 7.8×10^7

2) 6×10^1 7) 2.5×10^0 12) 2.2×10^{-6}

3) 2×10^6 8) 2.3×10^{-4} 13) 1.2×10^{-4}

4) 6×10^{-7} 9) 5.6×10^7 14) 4×10^{-3}

5) 3.54×10^5 10) 2×10^6 15) 7.8×10^1

16) 1.6×10^3

17) 1.45×10^3

18) 1.3×10^5

19) 6×10^1

20) 1.13×10^{-1}

21) 2×10^{-2}

Square Roots

1) 1

2) 2

3) 3

4) 5

5) 4

6) 7

7) 6

8) 0

9) 8

10) 9

11) 11

12) 15

13) 12

14) 10

15) 16

16) 17

17) 18

18) 20

19) 30

20) 23

21) $3\sqrt{10}$

Chapter 14: Statistics

Topics that you'll learn in this chapter:

- ✓ Mean, Median, Mode, and Range of the Given Data
- ✓ Box and Whisker Plots
- ✓ Bar Graph
- ✓ Stem– And– Leaf Plot
- ✓ The Pie Graph or Circle Graph
- ✓ Scatter Plots

Mathematics is no more computation than typing is literature.

– John Allen Paulos

Mean, Median, Mode, and Range of the Given Data

Mean, Median, Mode, and Range of the Given Data

Helpful Hints

- Mean: $\dfrac{\text{sum of the data}}{\text{of data entires}}$
- Mode: value in the list that appears most often
- Range: largest value − smallest value

Example:

22, 16, 12, 9, 7, 6, 4, 6

Mean = 10.25

Mod = 6

Range = 18

✍ **Find Mean, Median, Mode, and Range of the Given Data.**

1) 7, 2, 5, 1, 1, 2

2) 2, 2, 2, 3, 6, 3, 7, 4

3) 9, 4, 3, 1, 7, 9, 4, 6, 4

4) 8, 4, 2, 4, 3, 2, 4, 5

5) 8, 5, 7, 5, 7, 9, 8

6) 5, 1, 4, 4, 9, 2, 9, 2, 5, 1

7) 4, 1, 5, 9, 7, 7, 5, 4, 3, 5

8) 7, 5, 4, 9, 6, 7, 7, 5, 2

9) 2, 5, 5, 6, 2, 4, 7, 6, 4, 9

10) 10, 5, 2, 5, 4, 5, 8, 10

11) 5, 1, 5, 2, 2

12) 2, 3, 5, 9, 6

Box and Whisker Plots

Helpful Hints	Box–and–whisker plots display data including quartiles. - IQR – interquartile range shows the difference from Q1 to Q3. - Extreme Values are the smallest and largest values in a data set.

Example:

73, 84, 86, 95, 68, 67, 100, 94, 77, 80, 62, 79

Maximum: 100, Minimum: 62, Q_1: 70.5, Q_2: 79.5, Q_3: 90

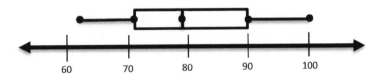

🖎 *Make box and whisker plots for the given data.*

11, 17, 22, 18, 23, 2, 3, 16, 21, 7, 8, 15, 5

Bar Graph

Helpful *Hints*	– A bar graph is a chart that presents data with bars in different heights to match with the values of the data. The bars can be graphed horizontally or vertically.

✍ *Graph the given information as a bar graph.*

Day	Hot dogs sold
Monday	90
Tuesday	70
Wednesday	30
Thursday	20
Friday	60

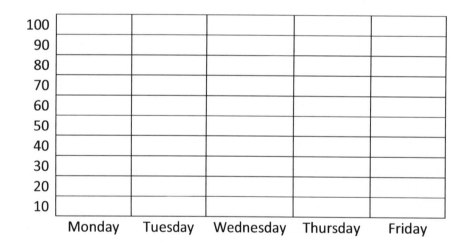

Stem–And–Leaf Plot

Helpful Hints	– Stem–and–leaf plots display the frequency of the values in a data set. – We can make a frequency distribution table for the values, or we can use a stem–and–leaf plot.

Example:

56, 58, 42, 48, 66, 64, 53, 69, 45, 72

Stem	leaf		
4	2	5	8
5	3	6	8
6	4	6	9
7	2		

✍ *Make stem ad leaf plots for the given data.*

1) 74, 88, 97, 72, 79, 86, 95, 79, 83, 91

Stem | Leaf plot

2) 37, 48, 26, 33, 49, 26, 19, 26, 48

Stem | Leaf plot

Stem | Leaf plot

3) 58, 41, 42, 67, 54, 65, 65, 54, 69, 53

The Pie Graph or Circle Graph

Helpful Hints	A Pie Chart is a circle chart divided into sectors, each sector represents the relative size of each value.

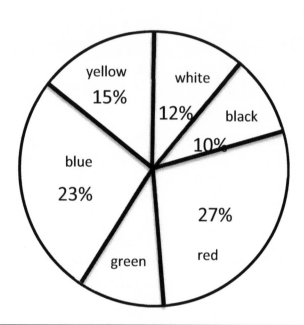

Favorite colors

1) Which color is the most popular?

2) What percentage of pie graph is yellow?

3) Which color is the least?

4) What percentage of pie graph is blue?

5) What percentage of pie graph is green?

Scatter Plots

Helpful	A Scatter (xy) Plot shows the values with points that represent the relationship between two sets of data.
Hints	– The horizontal values are usually x and vertical data is y.

✎ **Construct a scatter plot.**

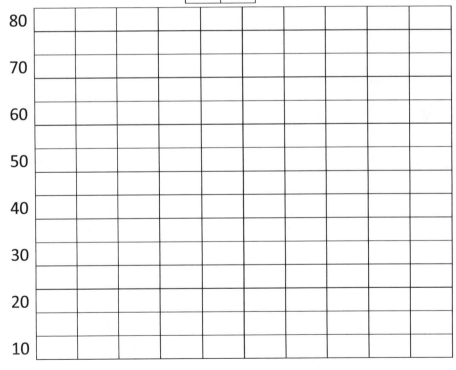

X	Y
1	20
2	40
3	50
4	60

Probability Problems

Helpful

Hints

- Probability is the likelihood of something happening in the future. It is expressed as a number between zero (can never happen) to 1 (will always happen).
- Probability can be expressed as a fraction, a decimal, or a percent.

Example:

Probability of a flipped coins turns up 'heads'

Is $0.5 = \dfrac{1}{2}$

✍ *Solve.*

1) A number is chosen at random from 1 to 10. Find the probability of selecting a 4 or smaller.

2) A number is chosen at random from 1 to 50. Find the probability of selecting multiples of 10.

3) A number is chosen at random from 1 to 10. Find the probability of selecting of 4 and factors of 6.

4) A number is chosen at random from 1 to 10. Find the probability of selecting a multiple of 3.

5) A number is chosen at random from 1 to 50. Find the probability of selecting prime numbers.

6) A number is chosen at random from 1 to 25. Find the probability of not selecting a composite number.

Answers of Worksheets – Chapter 14

Mean, Median, Mode, and Range of the Given Data

1) mean: 3, median: 2, mode: 1, 2, range: 6
2) mean: 3.625, median: 3, mode: 2, range: 5
3) mean: 5.22, median: 4, mode: 4, range: 8
4) mean: 4, median: 4, mode: 4, range: 6
5) mean: 7, median: 7, mode: 5, 7, 8, range: 4
6) mean: 4.2, median: 4, mode: 1,2,4,5,9, range: 8
7) mean: 5, median: 5, mode: 5, range: 8
8) mean: 5.78, median: 6, mode: 7, range: 7
9) mean: 5, median: 5, mode: 2, 4, 5, 6, range: 7
10) mean: 6.125, median: 5, mode: 5, range: 8
11) mean: 3, median: 2, mode: 2, 5, range: 4
12) mean: 5, median: 5, mode: none, range: 7

Box and Whisker Plots

11, 17, 22, 18, 23, 2, 3, 16, 21, 7, 8, 15, 5

Maximum: 23, Minimum: 2, Q_1: 2, Q_2: 12.5, Q_3: 19.5

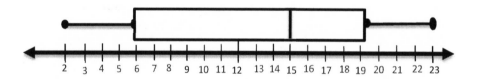

Bar Graph

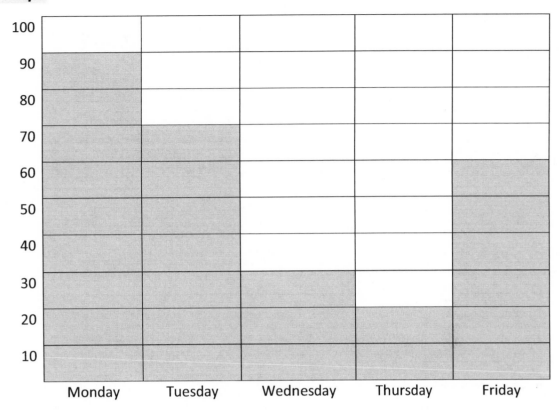

Stem–And–Leaf Plot

1)

Stem	leaf
7	2 4 9 9
8	3 6 8
9	1 5 7

2)

Stem	leaf
1	9
2	6 6 6
3	3 7
4	8 8 9

3)

Stem	leaf
4	1 2
5	3 4 4 8
6	5 5 7 9

The Pie Graph or Circle Graph

1) red
2) 15%

3) black
4) 23%

5) 13%

Scatter Plots

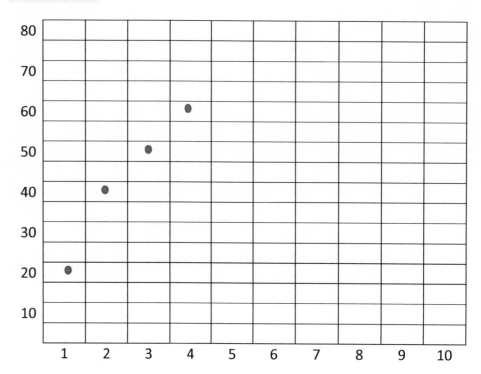

Probability Problems

1) $\frac{2}{5}$

3) $\frac{1}{2}$

5) $\frac{7}{25}$

2) $\frac{1}{10}$

4) $\frac{3}{10}$

6) $\frac{9}{25}$

Chapter 15: Geometry

Topics that you'll learn in this chapter:

- ✓ The Pythagorean Theorem
- ✓ Area of Triangles
- ✓ Perimeter of Polygons
- ✓ Area and Circumference of Circles
- ✓ Area of Squares, Rectangles, and Parallelograms
- ✓ Area of Trapezoids

Mathematics is, as it were, a sensuous logic, and relates to philosophy as do the arts, music, and plastic

art to poetry. — K. Shegel

The Pythagorean Theorem

Helpful	— In any right triangle:	Example:
Hints	$a^2 + b^2 = c^2$	Missing side = 6 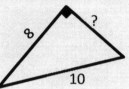

✎ **Do the following lengths form a right triangle?**

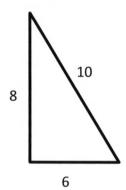

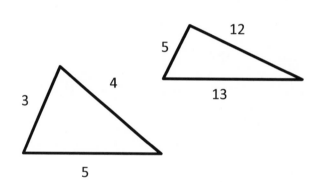

✎ **Find each missing length to the nearest tenth.**

4)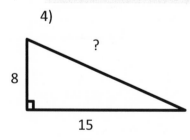

5)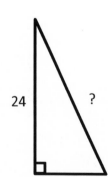

6)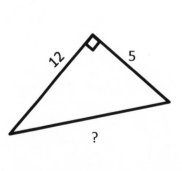

Area of Triangles

Helpful	$\text{Area} = \dfrac{1}{2}\ (base\ \times\ height)$
Hints	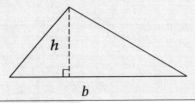

✏️ **Find the area of each.**

1)

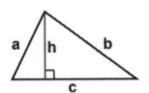

c = 9 mi

h = 3.7 mi

2)

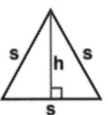

s = 14 m

h = 12.2 m

3)

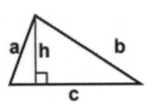

a = 5 m

b = 11 m

c = 14 m

h = 4 m

4)

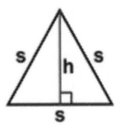

s = 10 m

h = 8.6 m

Perimeter of Polygons

Helpful

Hints

Perimeter of a square = 4s

  s

Perimeter of a rectangle

= $2(l + w)$

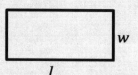 w

l

Perimeter of trapezoid

= a + b + c + d

a

d   b

c

Perimeter of Pentagon = 6a

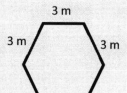 a

Perimeter of a parallelogram = 2(l + w)

l

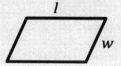 w

Example:

P = 18

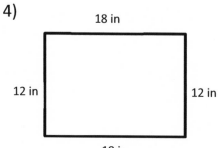

3 m

3 m   3 m

🖎 *Find the perimeter of each shape.*

1)

5 m

5 m   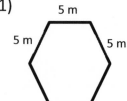 5 m

2)

15 mm

15 mm   15mm

15 mm

3)

12 ft   12 ft

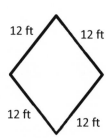

12 ft   12 ft

4)

18 in

12 in   12 in

18 in

Area and Circumference of Circles

Helpful *Hints*	Area = πr² Circumference = 2πr 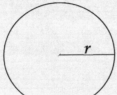	**Example:** If the radius of a circle is 3, then: Area = 28.27 Circumference = 18.85

✎ **Find the area and circumference of each.** (π = 3.14)

1)

2)

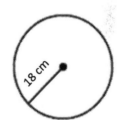

3)

4)

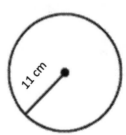

5)

6)

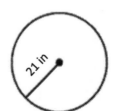

Area of Squares, Rectangles, and Parallelograms

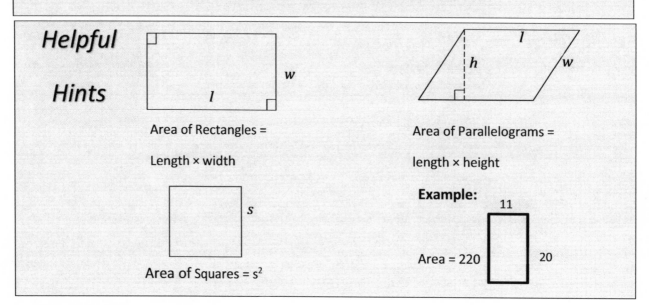

Helpful

Hints

Area of Rectangles =

Length × width

Area of Squares = s²

Area of Parallelograms =

length × height

Example:

11

Area = 220   20

✍ *Find the area of each.*

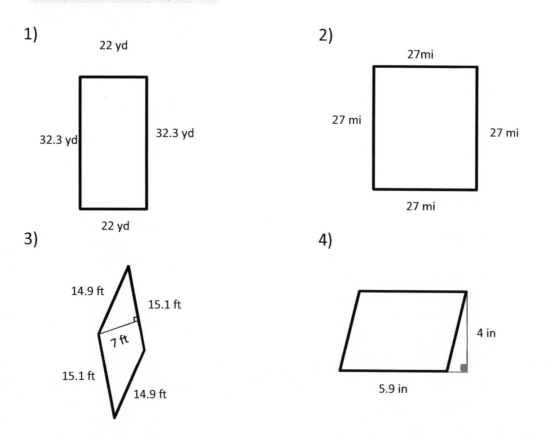

1)

22 yd

32.3 yd   32.3 yd

22 yd

2)

27mi

27 mi   27 mi

27 mi

3)

14.9 ft

15.1 ft

7 ft

15.1 ft

14.9 ft

4)

4 in

5.9 in

Area of Trapezoids

Helpful

Hints

$A = \frac{1}{2}h(b_1 + b_2)$

Example:

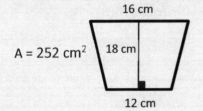

16 cm

18 cm

A = 252 cm²

12 cm

✎ **Calculate the area for each trapezoid.**

1)

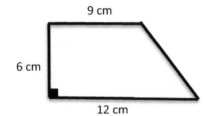

9 cm

6 cm

12 cm

2)

14 m

10 m

18 m

3)

22 mi

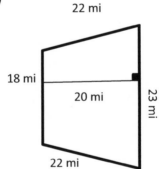

18 mi

20 mi

23 mi

22 mi

4)

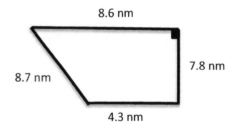

8.6 nm

8.7 nm

7.8 nm

4.3 nm

Answers of Worksheets – Chapter 15

The Pythagorean Theorem

1) yes
2) yes
3) yes

4) 17
5) 26
6) 13

Area of Triangles

1) 16.65 mi^2
2) 85.4 m^2

3) 28 m^2
4) 43 m^2

Perimeter of Polygons

1) 30 m
2) 60 mm

3) 48 ft
4) 60 in

Area and Circumference of Circles

1) Area: 50.24 in^2, Circumference: 25.12 in
2) Area: 1,017.36 cm^2, Circumference: 113.04 cm
3) Area: 78.5m^2, Circumference: 31.4 m
4) Area: 379.94 cm^2, Circumference: 69.08 cm
5) Area: 200.96 km^2, Circumference: 50.2 km
6) Area: 1,384.74 km^2, Circumference: 131.88 km

Area of Squares, Rectangles, and Parallelograms

1) 710.6 yd^2
2) 729 mi^2

3) 105.7 ft^2
4) 23.6 in^2

Area of Trapezoids

1) 63 cm^2
2) 160 m^2

3) 410 mi^2
4) 50.31 nm^2

Chapter 16: Solid Figures

Topics that you'll learn in this chapter:

- ✓ Volume of Cubes
- ✓ Volume of Rectangle Prisms
- ✓ Surface Area of Cubes
- ✓ Surface Area of Rectangle Prisms
- ✓ Volume of a Cylinder
- ✓ Surface Area of a Cylinder

Mathematics is a great motivator for all humans. Because its career starts with zero and it never end

(infinity)

Volume of Cubes

Helpful	– Volume is the measure of the amount of space inside of a solid figure, like a cube, ball, cylinder or pyramid.
Hints	– Volume of a cube = (one side)^3
	– Volume of a rectangle prism: Length × Width × Height

✎ *Find the volume of each.*

1)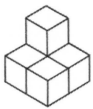

2)

3)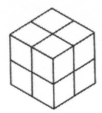

4)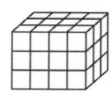

5)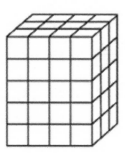

6)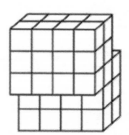

Volume of Rectangle Prisms

Helpful

Hints

Volume of rectangle prism

length × width × height

Example:

$10 × 5 × 8 = 400m^3$

10 m

8 m

5 m

✎ **Find the volume of each of the rectangular prisms.**

1)

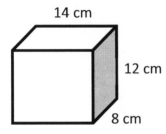

14 cm

12 cm

8 cm

2)

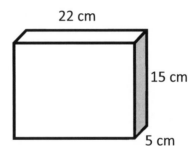

22 cm

15 cm

5 cm

3)

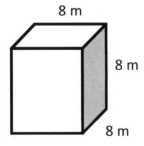

8 m

8 m

8 m

4)

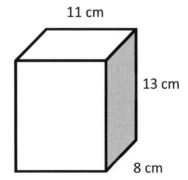

11 cm

13 cm

8 cm

Surface Area of Cubes

Helpful

Hints

Surface Area of a cube =

6 × (one side of the cube)^2

Example:

$6 \times 4^2 = 96m^2$

4 m

4 m

4 m

✎*Find the surface of each cube.*

1)

6 mm

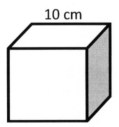

2)

9 mm

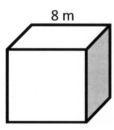

3)

10 cm

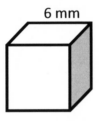

4)

8 m

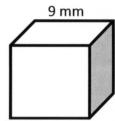

5)

7.5 in

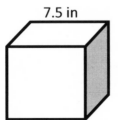

6)

11.3 ft

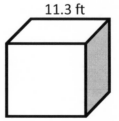

Surface Area of a Rectangle Prism

Helpful

Hints

Surface Area of a Rectangle Prism Formula:

SA =2 [(width × length) + (height × length) + width × height)]

✎ *Find the surface of each prism.*

1)

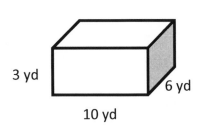

3 yd

6 yd

10 yd

2)

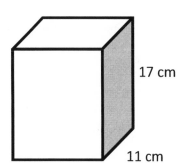

7 mm

7 mm

7 mm

3)

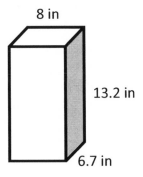

8 in

13.2 in

6.7 in

4)

17 cm

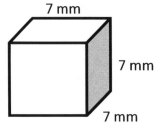

17 cm

11 cm

Volume of a Cylinder

✍ *Find the volume of each cylinder.* (π = 3.14)

1)

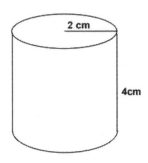

2 cm

4cm

2)

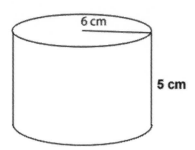

6 cm

5 cm

3)

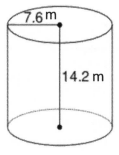

7.6 m

14.2 m

4)

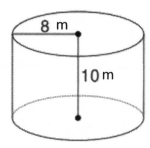

8 m

10 m

Surface Area of a Cylinder

Helpful		**Example:**
	Surface area of a cylinder	Surface area
Hints	$SA = 2\pi r^2 + 2\pi rh$	= 1727

14 m
11 m

✎ *Find the surface of each cylinder.* ($\pi = 3.14$)

1)

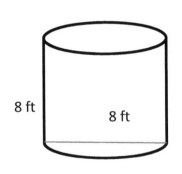

8 ft   8 ft

2)

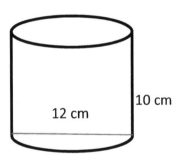

12 cm   10 cm

3)

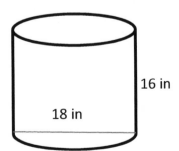

16 in
18 in

4)

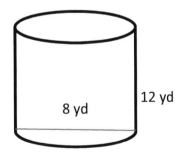

12 yd
8 yd

Answers of Worksheets – Chapter 16

Volumes of Cubes

1) 8
2) 4
3) 5
4) 36
5) 60
6) 44

Volume of Rectangle Prisms

1) 1344 cm^3
2) 1650 cm^3
3) 512 m^3
4) 1144 cm^3

Surface Area of a Cube

1) 216 mm^2
2) 486 mm^2
3) 600 cm^2
4) 384 m^2
5) 337.5 in^2
6) 766.14 ft^2

Surface Area of a Prism

1) 216 yd^2
2) 294 mm^2
3) 495.28 in^2
4) 1326 cm^2

Volume of a Cylinder

1) 50.24 cm^3
2) 565.2 cm^3
3) 2,575.403 m^3
4) 2009.6 m^3

Surface Area of a Cylinder

1) 301.44 ft^2
2) 602.88 cm^2
3) 1413 in^2
4) 401.92 yd^2

Chapter 17: Logarithms

Topics that you'll learn in this chapter:

- ✓ Rewriting Logarithms
- ✓ Evaluating Logarithms
- ✓ Properties of Logarithms
- ✓ Natural Logarithms
- ✓ Solving Exponential Equations Requiring Logarithms
- ✓ Solving Logarithmic Equations

Mathematics is an art of human understanding. — William Thurston

Rewriting Logarithms

Helpful	$\log_b y = x$	Example:
	is equivalent to	$\log_4 y = 3$
Hints	$y = b^x$	$y = 4^3$

✎ **Rewrite each equation in exponential form.**

1) $\log_{24} 15 = 0.85$

$24^{.85} = 15$

2) $\log_{320} 35 = 0.61$

$320^{.61} = 35$

3) $\log_7 49 = 2$

$7^2 = 49$

4) $\log_6 36 = 2$

$6^2 = 36$

✎ **Rewrite each equation in exponential form.**

5) $\log_a \frac{5}{8} = b$

$a^b = \frac{5}{8}$

6) $\log_x y = 6$

$x^6 = y$

7) $\log_{12} n = m$

$12^m = n$

8) $\log_y x = -8$

9) $\log_a b = 22$

10) $\log_{\frac{1}{5}} v = u$

✎ **Evaluate each expression.**

11) $\log_4 64 = x$

$4^x = 64$

$x = 3$

12) $\log_4 16 = x$

$4^x = 16$

$x = 2$

13) $\log_5 125 = x$

$5^x = 125 \quad x = 3$

14) $\log_9 3 = x$

$9^x = 3$

$x = \frac{1}{2}$

Evaluating Logarithms

Helpful

Hints

Change of Base Formula:

$$\log_b (x) = \frac{\log_d (x)}{\log_d (b)}$$

✎ *Evaluate each expression.*

1) $\log_3 27$

2) $\log_2 32$

3) $\log_4 16$

4) $\log_2 4$

5) $\log_8 64$

6) $\log_7 \frac{1}{49}$

7) $\log_{64} \frac{1}{4}$

8) $\log_{80} 700$

9) $\log_4 \frac{1}{64}$

10) $\log_5 625$

11) $\log_6 216$

12) $\log_8 \frac{1}{216}$

13) $\log_8 512$

14) $\log_7 2401$

Properties of Logarithms

Helpful

Hints

$a^{\log_a b} = b$

$\log_a 1 = 0$

$\log_a a = 1$

$\log_a(x \cdot y) = \log_a x + \log_a y$

$\log_a \frac{x}{y} = \log_a x - \log_a y$

$\log_a \frac{1}{x} = -\log_a x$

$\log_a x^p = p \log_a x$

$\log_{x^k} x = \frac{1}{x}\log_a x$, for $k \neq 0$

$\log_a x = \log_{a^c} x^c$

$\log_a x = \frac{1}{\log_x a}$

✎ **Expand each logarithm.**

1) $\log \left(\frac{2}{5}\right)^3$ $3 \log 2 - 3 \log 5$

2) $\log (2 \cdot 3^4)$ $\log 2 + 4 \log 3$

3) $\log \left(\frac{5}{7}\right)^4$ $4 \log 5 - 4 \log 7$

4) $\log \frac{2^3}{7}$ $3 \log 2 - \log 7$

5) $\log (x \cdot y)^5$ $5(\log x + \log y)$

6) $\log (8 \cdot 5)$

7) $\log (3 \cdot 7)$

8) $\log (x^3 \cdot y \cdot z^4)$

9) $\log \frac{u^4}{v}$

10) $\log \frac{x}{y^6}$

✎ **Condense each expression to a single logarithm.**

11) $\log 2 - \log 9$

12) $5 \log 6 - 3 \log 4$

13) $\log 7 - 2 \log 12$

14) $4 \log_5 a + 7 \log_5 b$

15) $2\log_3 x - 9 \log_3 y$

16) $\log_4 u - 6 \log_4 v$

17) $4 \log_6 u + 8 \log_6 v$

18) $4 \log_3 u - 20 \log_3 v$

Natural Logarithms

Helpful	$ln(x \cdot y) = ln(x) + ln(y)$
	$ln\left(\dfrac{x}{y}\right) = ln(x) - ln(y)$
Hints	$ln(x^y) = y \cdot ln(x)$

✎ *Solve.*

1) $e^x = 3$

2) $ln(lnx) = 5$

3) $e^x = 9$

4) $ln(2x + 5) = 4$

5) $ln(6x - 1) = 1$

6) $ln x = \dfrac{1}{2}$

7) $x = e^{\frac{1}{2}}$

8) $lnx = ln4 + ln7$

✎ *Evaluate without using a calculator.*

9) $ln 1$

10) $ln e^3$

11) $4 ln e$

12) $ln\left(\dfrac{1}{e}\right)$

13) e^{ln10}

14) e^{3ln2}

15) e^{5ln2}

16) $ln \sqrt{e}$

Solving Exponential Equations Requiring Logarithms

Helpful	if	$b^m = b^n$
Hints	then	$m = n$

✎ **Solve each equation.**

1) $4^{r+1} = 1$

2) $243^x = 81$

3) $6^{-3v-2} = 36$

4) $3^{2n} = 9$

5) $\dfrac{216^{2a}}{36^{-a}} = 216$

6) $25 \cdot 25^{-v} = 625$

7) $3^{2n} = 9$

8) $(\dfrac{1}{6})^n = 36$

9) $32^{2x} = 8$

10) $2^{-3x} = 2^{x-1}$

11) $2^{2n} = 16$

12) $5^{3n} = 125$

13) $3^{-2k} = 81$

14) $5^{3r} = 5^{-2r}$

15) $10^{3x} = 10000$

16) $25 \cdot 125^{-v} = 625$

17) $\dfrac{125}{25^{-3m}} = 25^{-2m-2}$

18) $2^{-2n} \cdot 2^{n+1} = 2^{-2n}$

Solving Logarithmic Equations

Helpful **Hints**	- Convert the logarithmic equation to an exponential equation when it's possible. (If no base is indicated, the base of the logarithm is 10)
	- Condense logarithms if you have more than one log on one side of the equation.
	- Plug in the answers back into the original equation and check to see the solution works.

✎ *Solve each equation.*

1) $2 \log_7 - 2x = 0$

2) $-\log_5 7x = 2$

3) $\log x + 5 = 2$

4) $\log x - \log 4 = 3$

5) $\log x + \log 2 = 4$

6) $\log 10 + \log x = 1$

7) $\log x + \log 8 = \log 48$

8) $-3 \log_3 (x - 2) = -12$

9) $\log 6x = \log (x + 5)$

10) $\log (4k - 5) = \log (2k - 1)$

11) $\log (4p - 2) = \log (-5p + 5)$

12) $-10 + \log_3 (n + 3) = -10$

13) $\log_9 (x + 2) = \log_9 (x^2 + 30)$ $x + 2 = x^2 + 30$ $x^2 - x + 28$

14) $\log_{12} (v^2 + 35) = \log_{12} (-2v - 1)$

15) $\log (16 + 2b) = \log (b^2 - 4b)$

16) $\log_9 (x + 6) - \log_9 x = \log_9 2$

17) $\log_5 6 + \log_5 2x^2 = \log_5 48$

18) $\log_6 (x + 1) - \log_6 x = \log_6 29$

Answers of Worksheets – Chapter 17

Rewriting Logarithms

1) $24^{0.85} = 15$

2) $320^{0.61} = 35$

3) $7^2 = 49$

4) $6^2 = 36$

5) $a^b = \dfrac{5}{8}$

6) $x^6 = y$

7) $12^m = n$

8) $y^{-8} = x$

9) $a^{22} = b$

10) $(\dfrac{1}{5})^u = v$

11) 3

12) 2

13) 3

14) $\dfrac{1}{2}$

Evaluating Logarithms

1) 3

2) 5

3) 2

4) 2

5) 2

6) −2

7) $-\dfrac{1}{3}$

8) 1.5

9) −3

10) 4

11) 3

12) −3

13) 3

14) 4

Properties of Logarithms

1) $3 \log 2 - 3 \log 5$

2) $\log 2 + 4 \log 3$

3) $4\log 5 - 4 \log 7$

4) $3 \log 2 - \log 7$

5) $5 \log x + 5 \log y$

6) $\text{Log } 8 + \log 5$

7) $\text{Log } 3 + \log 7$

8) $3\text{Log } x + \log y + 4 \log z$

9) $4 \log u - \log v$

10) $\text{Log } x - 6 \log y$

11) $\log \dfrac{2}{9}$

12) $\log \dfrac{6^5}{4^3}$

13) $\log \dfrac{7}{12^2}$

14) $\log_5 (a^4 b^7)$

15) $\log_3 \dfrac{x^2}{y^9}$

16) $\log_4 \dfrac{u}{v^6}$

17) $\log_6 (v^8 u^4)$

18) $\log_3 \dfrac{u^4}{v^{20}}$

Natural Logarithms

1) $x = \ln 3$
2) $x = e^{e^5}$
3) $x = \ln 9$
4) $x = \frac{e^2 - 5}{2}$
5) $x = \frac{e+1}{6}$

6) $\ln(e^{3-x}) = 8$
7) $x = -5$
8) $x = 28$
9) 0
10) 3
11) 4

12) −1
13) 10
14) 8
15) 32
16) $\frac{1}{2}$

Solving Exponential Equations Requiring Logarithms

1) $-\frac{1}{2}$
2) $\frac{1}{48}$
3) 95
4) 4000
5) 50
6) 1

7) 6
8) 83
9) 1
10) $\frac{1}{4}$
11) 2
12) 1
13) −2

14) 0
15) $\frac{4}{3}$
16) $-\frac{2}{3}$
17) $-\frac{7}{10}$
18) −1

Solving Logarithmic Equations

1) $\{-\frac{1}{2}\}$
2) $\{\frac{1}{35}\}$
3) $\{-100\}$
4) $\{20\}$
5) $\{\frac{25}{2}\}$
6) $\{5\}$

7) $\{\frac{37}{7}\}$
8) $\{84\}$
9) $\{3\}$
10) $\{2\}$
11) $\{\frac{7}{9}\}$
12) $\{-2\}$

13) $\{-7, -4\}$
14) $\{-6\}$
15) $\{8, -2\}$
16) $\{6\}$
17) $\{2, -2\}$
18) $\{\frac{1}{28}\}$

Chapter 18: Matrices

Topics that you'll learn in this chapter:

- ✓ Adding and Subtracting Matrices

- ✓ Matrix Multiplications

- ✓ Finding Determinants of a Matrix

- ✓ Finding Inverse of a Matrix

- ✓ Matrix Equations

Mathematics is an independent world created out of pure intelligence.

— William Woods Worth

Adding and Subtracting Matrices

Helpful	- We can add or subtract two matrices if they have the same dimensions.
Hints	- For addition or subtraction, add or subtract the corresponding entries, and place the result in the corresponding position in the resultant matrix.

✎ **Simplify.**

1) $|2 \quad -5 \quad -3| + |1 \quad -2 \quad -3|$

2) $\begin{vmatrix} 3 & 6 \\ -1 & -3 \\ -5 & -1 \end{vmatrix} + \begin{vmatrix} 0 & -1 \\ 6 & 0 \\ 2 & 3 \end{vmatrix}$

3) $\begin{vmatrix} -5 & 2 & -2 \\ 4 & -2 & 0 \end{vmatrix} - \begin{vmatrix} 6 & -5 & -6 \\ 1 & 3 & -3 \end{vmatrix}$

4) $|4 \quad 2| + |-2 \quad -6|$

5) $\begin{vmatrix} 2 \\ 4 \end{vmatrix} + \begin{vmatrix} 5 \\ 6 \end{vmatrix}$

6) $\begin{vmatrix} -4n & n+m \\ -2n & -4m \end{vmatrix} + \begin{vmatrix} 4 & -5 \\ 3m & 0 \end{vmatrix}$

7) $\begin{vmatrix} -6r+t \\ -r \\ 6s \end{vmatrix} + \begin{vmatrix} 6r \\ -4t \\ -3r+2 \end{vmatrix}$

8) $\begin{vmatrix} z-5 \\ -6 \\ -1-6z \\ 3y \end{vmatrix} + \begin{vmatrix} -3y \\ 3z \\ 5+z \\ 4z \end{vmatrix}$

9) $\begin{vmatrix} 8 & 7 \\ -6 & 5 \end{vmatrix} + \begin{vmatrix} 4 & -3 \\ 1 & 13 \end{vmatrix}$

10) $|-13 \quad 18 \quad 12| + |34 \quad -3 \quad 9|$

11) $\begin{vmatrix} 2 & -5 & 9 \\ 4 & -7 & 11 \\ -6 & 3 & -17 \end{vmatrix} + \begin{vmatrix} 3 & 4 & -5 \\ 13 & 2 & 5 \\ 4 & -8 & 1 \end{vmatrix}$

12) $\begin{vmatrix} 1 & -7 & 15 \\ 31 & 3 & 18 \\ 22 & 6 & 4 \end{vmatrix} + \begin{vmatrix} 13 & 17 & 5 \\ 3 & 8 & -1 \\ -9 & 2 & 12 \end{vmatrix}$

Matrix Multiplication

Helpful	- Step 1: Make sure that it's possible to multiply the two matrices (the number of columns in the 1st one should be the same as the number of rows in the second one.)
Hints	- Step 2: The elements of each row of the first matrix should be multiplied by the elements of each column in the second matrix.
	- Step 3: Add the products.

✏️ *Simplify.*

1) $\begin{vmatrix} -5 & -5 \\ -1 & 2 \end{vmatrix} \cdot \begin{vmatrix} -2 & -3 \\ 3 & 5 \end{vmatrix}$

2) $\begin{vmatrix} 0 & 5 \\ -3 & 1 \\ -5 & 1 \end{vmatrix} \cdot \begin{vmatrix} -4 & 4 \\ -2 & -4 \end{vmatrix}$

3) $\begin{vmatrix} 3 & 2 & 5 \\ 2 & 3 & 1 \end{vmatrix} \cdot \begin{vmatrix} 4 & 5 & -5 \\ 5 & -1 & 6 \end{vmatrix}$

4) $\begin{vmatrix} -5 \\ 6 \\ 0 \end{vmatrix} \cdot \begin{vmatrix} 3 & -1 \end{vmatrix}$

5) $\begin{vmatrix} 3 & -1 \\ -3 & 6 \\ -6 & -6 \end{vmatrix} \cdot \begin{vmatrix} -1 & 6 \\ 5 & 4 \end{vmatrix}$

6) $\begin{vmatrix} -2 & -6 \\ -4 & 3 \\ 5 & 0 \\ 4 & -6 \end{vmatrix} \cdot \begin{vmatrix} 2 & -2 & 2 \\ -2 & 0 & -3 \end{vmatrix}$

7) $\begin{vmatrix} -4 & -y \\ -2x & -4 \end{vmatrix} \cdot \begin{vmatrix} -4x & 0 \\ 2y & -5 \end{vmatrix}$

8) $\begin{vmatrix} 2 & -5v \end{vmatrix} \cdot \begin{vmatrix} -5u & -v \\ 0 & 6 \end{vmatrix}$

9) $\begin{vmatrix} -1 & 1 & -1 \\ 5 & 2 & -5 \\ 6 & -5 & 1 \\ -5 & 6 & 0 \end{vmatrix} \cdot \begin{vmatrix} 6 & 5 \\ 5 & -6 \\ 6 & 0 \end{vmatrix}$

10) $\begin{vmatrix} 5 & 3 & 5 \\ 1 & 5 & 0 \end{vmatrix} \cdot \begin{vmatrix} -4 & 2 \\ -3 & 4 \\ 3 & -5 \end{vmatrix}$

11) $\begin{vmatrix} -3 & 5 \\ -2 & 1 \end{vmatrix} \cdot \begin{vmatrix} 6 & -2 \\ 1 & -5 \end{vmatrix}$

12) $\begin{vmatrix} 0 & 2 \\ -2 & -5 \end{vmatrix} \cdot \begin{vmatrix} 6 & -6 \\ 3 & 0 \end{vmatrix}$

Finding Determinants of a Matrix

Helpful		
	$\begin{bmatrix} a & b \\ c & d \end{bmatrix}$	$\|A\| = ad - bc$
Hints	$\begin{bmatrix} a & b & c \\ d & e & f \\ g & h & i \end{bmatrix}$	$\|A\| = a(ei - fh) - b(di - fg) + c(dh - eg)$

✏ *Evaluate the determinant of each matrix.*

1) $\begin{vmatrix} 0 & -4 \\ -6 & -2 \end{vmatrix}$

2) $\begin{vmatrix} 5 & 3 \\ 6 & 6 \end{vmatrix}$

3) $\begin{vmatrix} -1 & 1 \\ -1 & 4 \end{vmatrix}$

4) $\begin{vmatrix} -9 & -9 \\ -7 & -10 \end{vmatrix}$

5) $\begin{vmatrix} -1 & 8 \\ 5 & 0 \end{vmatrix}$

6) $\begin{vmatrix} 8 & -6 \\ -10 & 9 \end{vmatrix}$

7) $\begin{vmatrix} 2 & -2 \\ 7 & -7 \end{vmatrix}$

8) $\begin{vmatrix} -5 & 0 \\ 3 & 10 \end{vmatrix}$

9) $\begin{vmatrix} 0 & 6 \\ -6 & 0 \end{vmatrix}$

10) $\begin{vmatrix} 0 & 4 \\ 6 & 5 \end{vmatrix}$

11) $\begin{vmatrix} -2 & 5 & -4 \\ 0 & -3 & 5 \\ -5 & 5 & -6 \end{vmatrix}$

12) $\begin{vmatrix} 5 & 3 & 3 \\ -4 & -5 & 1 \\ 5 & 3 & 0 \end{vmatrix}$

13) $\begin{vmatrix} 6 & 2 & -1 \\ -5 & -4 & -5 \\ 3 & -3 & 1 \end{vmatrix}$

14) $\begin{vmatrix} 6 & 5 & -3 \\ -5 & 4 & -2 \\ 1 & -4 & 5 \end{vmatrix}$

15) $\begin{vmatrix} -1 & -8 & 9 \\ 4 & 12 & -7 \\ -10 & 3 & 2 \end{vmatrix}$

Finding Inverse of a Matrix

Helpful

Hints
$$A = \begin{bmatrix} a & b \\ c & d \end{bmatrix} \qquad A^{-1} = \frac{1}{|A|} \begin{bmatrix} d & -b \\ -c & a \end{bmatrix}$$

✎ *Find the inverse of each matrix.*

1) $\begin{vmatrix} 3 & -2 \\ -4 & 6 \end{vmatrix}$

2) $\begin{vmatrix} 5 & -8 \\ 6 & -9 \end{vmatrix}$

3) $\begin{vmatrix} 2 & -10 \\ -11 & 8 \end{vmatrix}$

4) $\begin{vmatrix} -9 & -6 \\ -5 & -4 \end{vmatrix}$

5) $\begin{vmatrix} -3 & 3 \\ 8 & 7 \end{vmatrix}$

6) $\begin{vmatrix} -2 & 2 \\ -9 & 8 \end{vmatrix}$

7) $\begin{vmatrix} 3 & -2 \\ -4 & 6 \end{vmatrix}$

8) $\begin{vmatrix} -6 & 11 \\ -4 & 7 \end{vmatrix}$

9) $\begin{vmatrix} -1 & 7 \\ -1 & 7 \end{vmatrix}$

10) $\begin{vmatrix} 1 & -1 \\ -6 & -3 \end{vmatrix}$

11) $\begin{vmatrix} 11 & -5 \\ 2 & -1 \end{vmatrix}$

12) $\begin{vmatrix} 0 & -2 \\ -1 & -9 \end{vmatrix}$

13) $\begin{vmatrix} 0 & 0 \\ -6 & 4 \end{vmatrix}$

14) $\begin{vmatrix} -9 & -9 \\ -2 & -2 \end{vmatrix}$

Matrix Equations

Helpful

Hints

- In a matrix equation, a variable stands for a matrix.

- Matrix addition or scalar multiplication can be used to solve a matrix equation.

✎ *Solve each equation.*

1) $\begin{vmatrix} -1 & 2 \\ -6 & 10 \end{vmatrix} z = \begin{vmatrix} 6 \\ 22 \end{vmatrix}$

7) $\begin{vmatrix} -1 & 1 \\ 5 & -2 \end{vmatrix} C = \begin{vmatrix} 4 \\ -26 \end{vmatrix}$

2) $3x = \begin{vmatrix} 12 & -12 \\ 21 & -27 \end{vmatrix}$

8) $\begin{vmatrix} 4 & -2 \\ -7 & 2 \end{vmatrix} C = \begin{vmatrix} -6 \\ 12 \end{vmatrix}$

3) $\begin{vmatrix} 20 & -3 \\ 15 & -3 \end{vmatrix} = \begin{vmatrix} -6 & -5 \\ -5 & -4 \end{vmatrix} x$

9) $\begin{vmatrix} 2 & -3 \\ -5 & 5 \end{vmatrix} Z = \begin{vmatrix} -1 \\ 20 \end{vmatrix}$

4) $Y - \begin{vmatrix} -1 \\ -5 \\ 8 \\ 8 \end{vmatrix} = \begin{vmatrix} -6 \\ 6 \\ -16 \\ 0 \end{vmatrix}$

10) $\begin{vmatrix} -5 \\ 5 \\ -20 \end{vmatrix} = 5B$

11) $\begin{vmatrix} -10 \\ 4 \\ 3 \end{vmatrix} = y - \begin{vmatrix} 7 \\ -5 \\ -11 \end{vmatrix}$

5) $\begin{vmatrix} -1 & -9 \\ 0 & -1 \end{vmatrix} C = \begin{vmatrix} 11 \\ 2 \end{vmatrix}$

6) $\begin{vmatrix} -1 & -2 \\ 2 & 9 \end{vmatrix} B = \begin{vmatrix} -3 & -5 & 13 \\ 21 & 0 & -36 \end{vmatrix}$

12) $-4b - \begin{vmatrix} 5 \\ 2 \\ -6 \end{vmatrix} = \begin{vmatrix} -33 \\ -2 \\ -22 \end{vmatrix}$

Answers of Worksheets – Chapter 18

Adding and Subtracting Matrices

1) $\begin{vmatrix} 3 & -7 & -6 \end{vmatrix}$

2) $\begin{vmatrix} 3 & 5 \\ 5 & -3 \\ -3 & 2 \end{vmatrix}$

3) $\begin{vmatrix} -11 & 7 & 4 \\ 3 & -5 & 3 \end{vmatrix}$

4) $\begin{vmatrix} 2 & -4 \end{vmatrix}$

5) $\begin{vmatrix} 7 \\ 10 \end{vmatrix}$

6) $\begin{vmatrix} -4n+4 & n+m-5 \\ -2n+3m & -4m \end{vmatrix}$

7) $\begin{vmatrix} t \\ -r-4t \\ 6s-3r+2 \end{vmatrix}$

8) $\begin{vmatrix} z-5-3y \\ -6+3z \\ -4-5z \\ 3y+4z \end{vmatrix}$

9) $\begin{vmatrix} 12 & 4 \\ -5 & 18 \end{vmatrix}$

10) $\begin{vmatrix} 21 & 15 & 21 \end{vmatrix}$

11) $\begin{vmatrix} -1 & -9 & 14 \\ -9 & -9 & 6 \\ -6 & 11 & -18 \end{vmatrix}$

12) $\begin{vmatrix} 14 & 10 & 20 \\ 34 & 11 & 17 \\ 13 & 8 & 16 \end{vmatrix}$

Matrix Multiplication

1) $\begin{vmatrix} -5 & -10 \\ 8 & 13 \end{vmatrix}$

2) $\begin{vmatrix} -10 & -20 \\ 10 & -16 \\ 18 & -24 \end{vmatrix}$

3) Undefined

4) $\begin{vmatrix} -15 & 5 \\ 18 & -6 \\ 0 & 0 \end{vmatrix}$

5) $\begin{vmatrix} -8 & 14 \\ 33 & 6 \\ -24 & -60 \end{vmatrix}$

6) $\begin{vmatrix} 8 & 4 & 14 \\ -14 & 8 & -17 \\ 10 & -10 & 10 \\ 20 & -8 & 26 \end{vmatrix}$

9) $\begin{vmatrix} -7 & -11 \\ 10 & 13 \\ 17 & 60 \\ 0 & -61 \end{vmatrix}$

7) $\begin{vmatrix} 16x - 2y^2 & 5y \\ 8x^2 - 8y & 20 \end{vmatrix}$

10) $\begin{vmatrix} -14 & -3 \\ -19 & 22 \end{vmatrix}$

8) $\begin{vmatrix} -10u & -32v \end{vmatrix}$

11) $\begin{vmatrix} -13 & -19 \\ -11 & -1 \end{vmatrix}$

12) $\begin{vmatrix} 6 & 0 \\ -27 & 12 \end{vmatrix}$

Finding Determinants of a Matrix

1) −24

2) 12

3) −3

4) 27

5) −40

6) 12

7) 0

8) −50

9) −36

10) −24

11) −51

12) 39

13) −161

14) 139

15) 647

Finding Inverse of a Matrix

1) $\begin{vmatrix} \dfrac{3}{5} & \dfrac{1}{5} \\ \dfrac{2}{5} & \dfrac{3}{10} \end{vmatrix}$

2) $\begin{vmatrix} -3 & \dfrac{8}{3} \\ -2 & \dfrac{5}{3} \end{vmatrix}$

3) $\begin{vmatrix} -\dfrac{4}{47} & -\dfrac{5}{47} \\ -\dfrac{2}{94} & -\dfrac{1}{47} \end{vmatrix}$

4) $\begin{vmatrix} -\dfrac{2}{3} & 1 \\ \dfrac{5}{6} & -\dfrac{3}{2} \end{vmatrix}$

5) $\begin{vmatrix} -\dfrac{7}{45} & \dfrac{1}{15} \\ \dfrac{8}{45} & \dfrac{1}{15} \end{vmatrix}$

6) $\begin{vmatrix} 4 & -1 \\ \dfrac{9}{2} & -1 \end{vmatrix}$

7) $\begin{vmatrix} \dfrac{3}{5} & \dfrac{1}{5} \\ \dfrac{2}{5} & \dfrac{3}{10} \end{vmatrix}$

8) $\begin{vmatrix} \dfrac{7}{2} & -\dfrac{11}{2} \\ 2 & -3 \end{vmatrix}$

9) No inverse exists

10) $\begin{vmatrix} \frac{1}{3} & -\frac{1}{9} \\ -\frac{2}{3} & -\frac{1}{9} \end{vmatrix}$

11) $\begin{vmatrix} 1 & -5 \\ 2 & -11 \end{vmatrix}$

12) $\begin{vmatrix} \frac{9}{2} & -1 \\ -\frac{1}{2} & 0 \end{vmatrix}$

13) No inverse exists

14) No inverse exists

Matrix Equations

1) $\begin{vmatrix} 8 \\ 7 \end{vmatrix}$

2) $\begin{vmatrix} 4 & -4 \\ 7 & -9 \end{vmatrix}$

3) $\begin{vmatrix} 5 & 3 \\ -10 & -3 \end{vmatrix}$

4) $\begin{vmatrix} -7 \\ 1 \\ -8 \\ 8 \end{vmatrix}$

5) $\begin{vmatrix} 7 \\ -2 \end{vmatrix}$

6) $\begin{vmatrix} -3 & 9 & -9 \\ 3 & -2 & -2 \end{vmatrix}$

7) $\begin{vmatrix} -6 \\ -2 \end{vmatrix}$

8) $\begin{vmatrix} -2 \\ -1 \end{vmatrix}$

9) $\begin{vmatrix} -11 \\ -7 \end{vmatrix}$

10) $\begin{vmatrix} -1 \\ 1 \\ -4 \end{vmatrix}$

11) $\begin{vmatrix} -3 \\ -1 \\ -8 \end{vmatrix}$

12) $\begin{vmatrix} 7 \\ 0 \\ 7 \end{vmatrix}$

Chapter 19: Functions Operations

Topics that you'll learn in this chapter:

- ✓ Relations and Functions
- ✓ Function Notation
- ✓ Adding and Subtracting Functions
- ✓ Multiplying and Dividing Functions
- ✓ Composition of Functions

Millions saw the apple fall, but Newton asked why." – Bernard Baruch

Function Notation

Helpful *Hints*	Function notation is the way a function is written. It is meant to be a precise way of giving information about the function without a rather lengthy written explanation. The most popular function notation is $f(x)$ which is read "f of x".	**Example:** $f = 12x$ $f(x)\ 12x$

✏️ **Write in function notation.**

1) d = 22t

2) c = p^2 + 5p + 5

3) m = 25n − 120

4) y = 2x − 6

✏️ **Evaluate each function.**

5) w(x) = 3x + 1, find w(4)

6) $h(n)$ = n^2 − 10, find h(5)

7) $h(x)$ = x^3 + 8, find h(−2)

8) $h(n)$ = − $2n^2$ − 6n, find h(2)

9) $g(n)$ = $3n^2$ + 2n, find g(2)

10) $g(n)$ = 10n − 3, find g(6)

11) g(n) = 8n + 4, find g(1)

12) h(x) = 4x − 22, find h(2)

13) $h(a)$ = − 11a+ 5, find $h(2a)$

14) $k(a)$ = 7a + 3, find $k(a − 2)$

15) $h(x)$ = 3x + 5, find $h(6x)$

16) $h(x)$ = x^2 + 1, find $h(\frac{x}{4})$

Adding and Subtracting Functions

Helpful

Hints

Just like we can add and subtract numbers, we can add and subtract functions. For example, if we had functions f and g, we could create two new functions: $f + g$ and $f - g$.

Example:

$f(x) = 12x$

$g(x) = x^2 + 3x$

$(f + g)(x) = f(x) + g(x) =$

$12x + x^2 + 3x$

$x^2 + 15x$

✎ *Perform the indicated operation.*

1) $h(t) = 2t + 1$
   $g(t) = 2t + 2$
   Find $(h - g)(t)$

2) $g(a) = -3^a - 3$
   f(a) $= a^2 + 5$
   Find $(g - f)(a)$

3) $g(x) = 2x - 5$
   $h(x) = 4x + 5$
   Find $g(3) - h(3)$

4) $h(3) = 3x + 3$
   $g(x) = -4x + 1$
   Find $(h + g)(10)$

5) $f(x) = 4x - 3$
   $g(x) = x^3 + 2x$
   Find $(f - g)(4)$

6) $h(n) = 4n + 5$
   g(n) $= 3n + 4$
   Find $(h - g)(n)$

7) $g(x) = -x^2 - 1 - 2x$
   $f(x) = 5 + x$
   Find $(g - f)(x)$

8) $g(t) = 2t + 5$
   $f(t) = -t^2 + 5$
   Find $(g + f)(t)$

Multiplying and Dividing Functions

Helpful *Hints*	Just like we can multiply and divide numbers, we can multiply and divide functions. For example, if we had functions f and g, we could create two new functions	**Example:**
	$f \cdot g$, and $\dfrac{f}{g}$.	$f(x) = 2x$ $g(x) = x^2 + x$ $(f \cdot g)(x) =$ $f(x) \cdot g(x) =$ $2x^3 + 2x^2$

✎ *Perform the indicated operation.*

1) $g(a) = 2a - 1$

   $h(a) = 3a - 3$

   Find $(g.h)(-4)$

2) $f(x) = 2x^3 - 5x^2$

   $g(x) = 2x - 1$

   Find $(f.g)(x)$

3) $g(t) = t^2 + 3$

   $h(t) = 4t - 3$

   Find $(g.h)(-1)$

4) $g(n) = n^2 + 4 + 2n$

   $h(n) = -3n + 2$

   Find $(g.h)(1)$

5) $g(a) = 3a + 2$

   $f(a) = 2a - 4$

   Find $(\dfrac{g}{f})(3)$

6) $f(x) = 3x - 1$

   $g(x) = x^2 - x$

   Find $(\dfrac{f}{g})(x)$

Composition of Functions

Helpful

Hints

The term "composition of functions" (or "composite function") refers to the combining together of two or more functions in a manner where the output from one function becomes the input for the next function.

The notation used for composition is: $(f \circ g)(x) = f(g(x))$

Example:

Using $f(x) = x + 1$ and $g(x) = 2x$, find:
$(f \circ g)(1)$

$(f \circ g)(x) = 2x + 1$

$(f \circ g)(1) = 3$

✎ *Using* f(x) = 5x + 4 *and* g(x) = x − 3, *find:*

1) $f(g(6))$

2) $f(f(8))$

3) $g(f(-7))$

4) $g(f(x))$

✎ *Using* f(x) = 6x + 2 *and* g(x) = x − 5, *find:*

5) $f(g(7))$

6) $f(f(2))$

7) $g(f(3))$

8) $g(g(x))$

✎ *Using* f(x) = 7x + 4 *and* g(x) = 2x − 4, *find:*

9) $f(g(3))$

10) $f(f(3))$

11) $g(f(4))$

12) $g(g(5))$

Answers of Worksheets – Chapter 19

Function Notation

1) $d(t) = 22t$
2) $c(p) = p^2 + 5p + 5$
3) $m(n) = 25n - 120$
4) $f(x) = 2x - 6$
5) 13
6) 15
7) 0
8) -20
9) 16
10) 57
11) 12
12) -8
13) $-22a + 5$
14) $7a - 11$
15) $18x + 5$
16) $1 + \dfrac{1}{16}x^2$

Adding and Subtracting Functions

1) -1
2) $-a^2 - 3a - 8$
3) -16
4) -6
5) -59
6) $n + 1$
7) $-x^2 - 3x - 6$
8) $-t^2 + 2t + 10$

Multiplying and Dividing Functions

1) 135
2) $4x^4 - 12x^3 + 5x^2$
3) -28
4) -7
5) $\dfrac{11}{2}$
6) $\dfrac{3x-1}{x^2-x}$

Composition of Functions

1) 19
2) 224
3) -34
4) $5x + 1$
5) 14
6) 86
7) 15
8) $x - 10$
9) 18
10) 179
11) 60
12) 8

Chapter 20: Trigonometric Functions

Topics that you'll learn in this chapter:

- ✓ Trig ratios of General Angles
- ✓ Sketch Each Angle in Standard Position
- ✓ Finding Co–Terminal Angles and Reference Angles
- ✓ Writing Each Measure in Radians
- ✓ Writing Each Measure in Degrees
- ✓ Evaluating Each Trigonometric Expression
- ✓ Missing Sides and Angles of a Right Triangle
- ✓ Arc Length and Sector Area

Mathematics is like checkers in being suitable for the young, not too difficult, amusing, and without peril

to the state. — Plato

Trig ratios of General Angles

θ	0°	30°	45°	60°	90°
$\sin\theta$	0	$\frac{1}{2}$	$\frac{\sqrt{2}}{2}$	$\frac{\sqrt{3}}{2}$	1
$\cos\theta$	1	$\frac{\sqrt{3}}{2}$	$\frac{\sqrt{2}}{2}$	$\frac{1}{2}$	0
$\tan\theta$	0	$\frac{\sqrt{3}}{3}$	1	$\sqrt{3}$	undefined

Helpful Hints

✎**Use a calculator to find each. Round your answers to the nearest ten–thousandth.**

1) $\sin -120°$

2) $\sin 150°$

3) $\cos 315°$

4) $\cos 180°$

5) $\sin 120°$

6) $\sin -330°$

✎**Find the exact value of each trigonometric function. Some may be undefined.**

7) $\sec 0$

8) $\tan -\frac{3\pi}{2}$

9) $\cos \frac{11\pi}{6}$

10) $\cot \frac{5\pi}{3}$

11) $\sec -\frac{3\pi}{4}$

12) $\tan \frac{2\pi}{3}$

196

Sketch Each Angle in Standard Position

Helpful *Hints*	- The standard position of an angle is when its vertex is located at the origin and its initial side extends along the positive x-axis. - A positive angle is the angle measured in a counterclockwise direction from the initial side to the terminal side. - A negative angle is the angle measured in a clockwise direction from the initial side to the terminal side.

✍ **Draw the angle with the given measure in standard position.**

1) −120°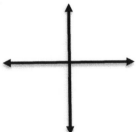

2) 440°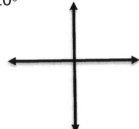

3) $-\frac{10\pi}{3}$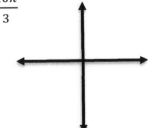

4) 280°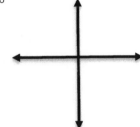

5) 710°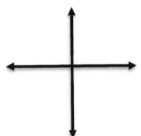

6) $\frac{11\pi}{6}$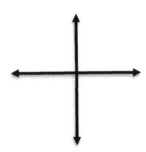

Finding Co-terminal Angles and Reference Angles

Helpful *Hints*	- Co-terminal angles are equal angles. - To find a co-terminal of an angle, add or subtract 360 degrees (or 2π for radians) to the given angle. - Reference angle is the smallest angle that you can make from the terminal side of an angle with the x-axis.

✎ *Find a conterminal angle between 0° and 360°.*

1) $-440°$

3) $-435°$

2) $640°$

4) $-330°$

✎ *Find a conterminal angle between 0 and 2π for each given angle.*

5) $\dfrac{15}{4}$

7) $-\dfrac{35}{18}$

6) $-\dfrac{19\pi}{12}$

8) $\dfrac{11\pi}{3}$

✎ *Find the reference angle.*

9)

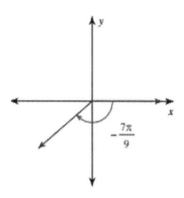

$-\dfrac{7\pi}{9}$

10)

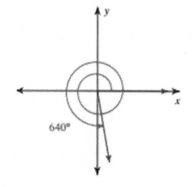

640°

Writing Each Measure in Radians

Helpful		Example:
Helpful	$radians = degrees \times \dfrac{\pi}{180}$	Convert 150 degrees to radians.
Hints		$radians = 150 \times \dfrac{\pi}{180} = \dfrac{5\pi}{6}$

✎ **Convert each degree measure into radians.**

1) −140°

2) 320°

3) 210°

4) 970°

5) −190°

6) 345°

7) 265°

8) 555°

9) 300°

10) 50°

11) 315°

12) 600°

13) 712°

14) −160°

15) −210°

16) 545°

17) −30°

18) 660°

19) −170°

20) 230°

21) 150°

Writing Each Measure in Degrees

Helpful		**Example:**
	$Degrees = radians \times \dfrac{180}{\pi}$	Convert $\dfrac{2\pi}{3}$ to degrees.
Hints		$\dfrac{2\pi}{3} \times \dfrac{180}{\pi} = \dfrac{360\pi}{3\pi} = 120$

✍ *Convert each radian measure into degrees.*

1) $\dfrac{\pi}{30}$

2) $\dfrac{32\pi}{40}$

3) $\dfrac{14\pi}{36}$

4) $\dfrac{\pi}{5}$

5) $-\dfrac{10}{8}$

6) $\dfrac{14}{3}$

7) $-\dfrac{16\pi}{3}$

8) $-\dfrac{50}{14}$

9) $\dfrac{11\pi}{6}$

10) $\dfrac{5\pi}{9}$

11) $-\dfrac{\pi}{3}$

12) $\dfrac{13\pi}{6}$

13) $\dfrac{15\pi}{20}$

14) $\dfrac{21}{4}$

15) $-\dfrac{68\pi}{45}$

16) $\dfrac{14\pi}{3}$

17) $-\dfrac{41\pi}{12}$

18) $-\dfrac{17\pi}{9}$

19) $\dfrac{35\pi}{18}$

20) $-\dfrac{3\pi}{2}$

21) $\dfrac{4\pi}{9}$

Evaluating Each Trigonometric Function

Helpful	- Step 1: Draw the terminal side of the angle. · - Step 2: Find reference angle. (It is the smallest angle that you can make from the terminal side of an angle with the x-axis.) - Step 3: Find the trigonometric function of the reference angle.
Hints	

✍ *Find the exact value of each trigonometric function.*

1) $\cos 225°$

2) $\tan \dfrac{7\pi}{6}$

3) $\tan -\dfrac{\pi}{6}$

4) $\cot -\dfrac{7\pi}{6}$

5) $\cos -\dfrac{\pi}{4}$

6) $\cos -480°$

7) $\sin 690°$

8) $\tan 420°$

9) $\cot -495°$

10) $\tan 405°$

✍ *Use the given point on the terminal side of angle θ to find the value of the trigonometric function indicated.*

11) $\sin \theta;\ (-6, 4)$

12) $\cos \theta;\ (2, -2)$

13) $\cot \theta;\ (-7, \sqrt{15})$

14) $\cos \theta;\ (-2\sqrt{3}, -2)$

15) $\sin \theta;\ (-\sqrt{7}, 3)$

16) $\tan \theta;\ (-11, -2)$

Missing Sides and Angles of a Right Triangle

Helpful	SOH − CAH - TOA
Hints	$sine\ \theta = \dfrac{opposite}{hypotenus}, Cos\ \theta = \dfrac{adjacent}{hypotenus}, \tan \theta = \dfrac{opposite}{adjacent}$

✍ **Find the value of each trigonometric ratio as fractions in their simplest form.**

1) tan A

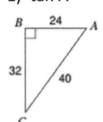

2) sin X

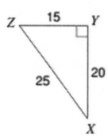

✍ **Find the missing side. Round answers to the nearest tenth.**

3)

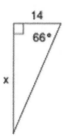

4)

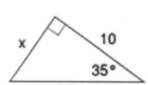

5)

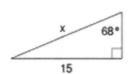

6)

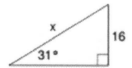

Arc Length and Sector Area

Helpful	$Area\ of\ a\ sector = \dfrac{1}{2}r^2\theta$
Hints	$length\ of\ a\ sector = (\dfrac{\theta}{180})\pi r$

✎ **Find the length of each arc. Round your answers to the nearest tenth.**

1) r = 28 cm, θ = 45°

3) r = 22 ft, θ = 60°

2) r = 15 ft, θ = 95°

4) r = 12 m, θ = 85°

✎ **Find area of a sector. Do not round.**

5)

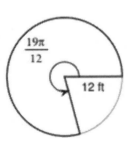

7)

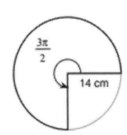

6)

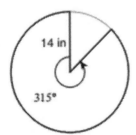

8)

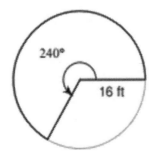

Answers of Worksheets – Chapter 20

Trig Ratios of General Angles

1) $-\frac{\sqrt{3}}{2}$

2) $\frac{1}{2}$

3) $-\frac{\sqrt{2}}{2}$

4) -1

5) $\frac{\sqrt{3}}{2}$

6) $\frac{1}{2}$

7) 1

8) Undefined

9) $\frac{\sqrt{3}}{2}$

10) $-\frac{\sqrt{3}}{3}$

11) $-\sqrt{2}$

12) $-\sqrt{3}$

Sketch Each Angle in Standard Position

1) −120∘

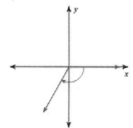

4) 280∘

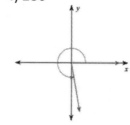

2) 440∘

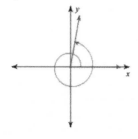

5) 710∘

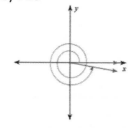

3) $-\frac{10\pi}{3}$

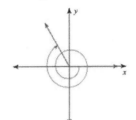

6) $\frac{11\pi}{6}$

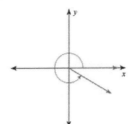

Finding Co–Terminal Angles and Reference Angles

1) 280°

2) 280°

3) 285°

4) 30°

5) $\frac{7\pi}{4}$

6) $\frac{5\pi}{12}$

7) $\frac{\pi}{18}$

8) $\frac{5\pi}{3}$

9) $\frac{2\pi}{9}$

10) 80°

Writing Each Measure in Radians

1) $-\frac{7\pi}{9}$

2) $\frac{16\pi}{9}$

3) $\frac{7\pi}{6}$

4) $\frac{97\pi}{18}$

5) $-\frac{19\pi}{18}$

6) $\frac{23\pi}{12}$

7) $\frac{53\pi}{36}$

8) $\frac{37\pi}{12}$

9) $\frac{5\pi}{3}$

10) $\frac{5\pi}{18}$

11) $\frac{7\pi}{4}$

12) $\frac{10\pi}{3}$

13) $\frac{178\pi}{45}$

14) $-\frac{8\pi}{9}$

15) $-\frac{7\pi}{6}$

16) $\frac{109\pi}{36}$

17) $-\frac{\pi}{6}$

18) $\frac{11\pi}{3}$

19) $-\frac{17\pi}{18}$

20) $\frac{23}{18}$

21) $\frac{5\pi}{6}$

Writing Each Measure in Degrees

1) 6°

2) 144°

3) 70°

4) 36°

5) −225°

6) 840°

7) −960°

8) −643°

9) 330°

10) 100°

11) −60°

12) 390°

13) 135°

14) 945°

15) −272°

16) 840°

17) −615°

18) −340°

19) 350°

20) −270°

21) 80°

Evaluating Each Trigonometric Expression

1) $-\dfrac{\sqrt{2}}{2}$

2) $\dfrac{\sqrt{3}}{3}$

3) $-\dfrac{\sqrt{3}}{3}$

4) $-\sqrt{3}$

5) $\dfrac{\sqrt{2}}{2}$

6) $-\dfrac{1}{2}$

7) $-\dfrac{1}{2}$

8) $\sqrt{3}$

9) 1

10) 1

11) $\dfrac{2\sqrt{13}}{13}$

12) $-\sqrt{2}$

13) $-\dfrac{7\sqrt{15}}{15}$

14) $-\dfrac{\sqrt{3}}{2}$

15) $\dfrac{3}{4}$

16) $\dfrac{2}{11}$

Missing Sides and Angles of a Right Triangle

1) $\dfrac{4}{3}$

2) $\dfrac{3}{5}$

3) 31.4

4) 7.0

5) 16.2

6) 31.1

Arc Length and Sector Area

1) 22 cm

2) 25 ft

3) 23 ft

4) 18 m

5) 114π ft²

6) $\dfrac{343\pi}{2}$ in²

7) 147π cm²

8) $\dfrac{512\pi}{3}$ ft²

206

Chapter 21: Sequences and Series

Topics that you'll learn in this chapter:

- ✓ Arithmetic Sequences
- ✓ Geometric Sequences
- ✓ Comparing Arithmetic and Geometric Sequences
- ✓ Finite Geometric Series
- ✓ Infinite Geometric Series

Mathematics is like checkers in being suitable for the young, not too difficult, amusing, and without

peril to the state. — Plato

Arithmetic Sequences

Helpful	$x_n = a + d(n-1)$
Hints	a = the first term d = the common difference between terms n = how many terms to add up

✒️ **Given the first term and the common difference of an arithmetic sequence find the first five terms and the explicit formula.**

1) $a_1 = 24, d = 2$

2) $a_1 = -15, d = -5$

3) $a_1 = 18, d = 10$

4) $a_1 = -38, d = -100$

✒️ **Given a term in an arithmetic sequence and the common difference find the first five terms and the explicit formula.**

5) $a_{36} = -276, d = -7$

6) $a_{37} = 249, d = 8$

7) $a_{38} = -53.2, d = -1.1$

8) $a_{40} = -1191, d = -30$

✒️ **Given a term in an arithmetic sequence and the common difference find the recursive formula and the three terms in the sequence after the last one given.**

9) $a_{22} = -44, d = -2$

10) $a_{12} = 28.6, d = 1.8$

11) $a_{18} = 27.4, d = 1.1$

12) $a_{21} = -1.4, d = 0.6$

Geometric Sequences

Helpful

Hints

$x_n = ar^{(n-1)}$

a = the first term
r = the common ratio

✍ *Determine if the sequence is geometric. If it is, find the common ratio.*

1) $1, -5, 25, -125, \ldots$

2) $-2, -4, -8, -16, \ldots$

3) $4, 16, 36, 64, \ldots$

4) $-3, -15, -75, -375, \ldots$

✍ *Given the first term and the common ratio of a geometric sequence find the first five terms and the explicit formula.*

5) $a_1 = 0.8, r = -5$

6) $a_1 = 1, r = 2$

✍ *Given the recursive formula for a geometric sequence find the common ratio, the first five terms, and the explicit formula.*

7) $a_n = a_{n-1} \cdot 2, a_1 = 2$

8) $a_n = a_{n-1} \cdot -3, a_1 = -3$

9) $a_n = a_{n-1} \cdot 5, a_1 = 2$

10) $a_n = a_{n-1} \cdot 3, a_1 = -3$

✍ *Given two terms in a geometric sequence find the 8th term and the recursive formula.*

11) $a_4 = 12$ and $a_5 = -6$

12) $a_5 = 768$ and $a_2 = 12$

Comparing Arithmetic and Geometric Sequences

Helpful Hints	Arithmetic Sequence: There is a constant difference between consecutive terms. (each term is the sum of previous term and a constant.
	Geometric Sequence: The consecutive terms are in a constant ratio. (each term is the product of previous term and a ratio)

✍ **For each sequence, state if it arithmetic, geometric, or neither.**

1) 1, 4, 9, 16, 25, …

2) 1, 5, 25, 125, 625, …

3) 4, 36, 64, 100, …

4) −29, −34, −39, −44, −49, …

5) −4, 12, −36, 108, −324, …

6) 40, 43, 46, 49, 52, …

7) 1, 3, 6, 10, 15, …

8) −34, −26, −18, −10, −2, …

9) $a_n = -163 + 200_n$

10) $a_n = 16 + 3_n$

11) $a_n = -4 \cdot (-3)^{n-1}$

12) $a_n = -43 + 4_n$

13) $a_n = (2n)^2$

14) $a_n = -43 + 7_n$

15) $a_n = -(-3)^{n-1}$

16) $a_n = 2 \cdot (-3)^{n-1}$

Finite Geometric Series

Helpful	Finite Geometric Series: The sum of a geometric series is finite when the absolute value of the ratio is less than 1.
Hints	$S_n = \sum_{i=1}^{n} ar^{i-1} = a_1(\frac{1-r^n}{1-r})$

✎ *Evaluate the related series of each sequence.*

1) $-1, 5, -25, 125$

3) $-1, 4, -16, 64$

2) $-2, 6, -18, 54, -162$

4) $2, 12, 72, 432$

✎ *Evaluate each geometric series described.*

5) $1 + 2 + 4 + 8 \dots, n = 6$

10) $-3 -6 -12 - 24 \dots, n = 9$

6) $1 - 4 + 16 - 64 \dots, n = 9$

11) $\sum_{n=1}^{8} 2 \cdot (-2)^{n-1}$

7) $-2 - 6 - 18 - 54 \dots, n = 9$

12) $\sum_{n=1}^{9} 4 \cdot 3^{n-1}$

8) $2 - 10 + 50 - 250 \dots, n = 8$

13) $\sum_{n=1}^{10} 4 \cdot (-3)^{n-1}$

9) $1 - 5 + 25 - 125 \dots, n = 7$

14) $\sum_{m=1}^{9} -2^{m-1}$

Infinite Geometric Series

Helpful Hints	Infinite Geometric Series: The sum of a geometric series is infinite when the absolute value of the ratio is more than 1. $$S = \sum_{i=0}^{\infty} a_i r^i = \frac{a_1}{1-r}$$

✎ **Determine if each geometric series converges or diverges.**

1) $a_1 = -3, r = 4$

2) $a_1 = 5.5, r = 0.5$

3) $a_1 = -1, r = 3$

4) $81 + 27 + 9 + 3 \dots,$

5) $-3 + \frac{12}{5} - \frac{48}{25} + \frac{192}{125} \dots,$

6) $\frac{128}{3125} - \frac{64}{625} + \frac{32}{125} - \frac{16}{25} \dots,$

✎ **Evaluate each infinite geometric series described.**

7) $a_1 = 3, r = -\frac{1}{5}$

8) $a_1 = 1, r = -3$

9) $a_1 = 1, r = -4$

10) $a_1 = 3, r = \frac{1}{2}$

11) $1 + 0.5 + 0.25 + 0.125 + \dots$

12) $81 - 27 + 9 - 3 \dots,$

13) $1 - 0.6 + 0.36 - 0.216 \dots,$

14) $3 + \frac{9}{4} + \frac{27}{16} + \frac{81}{64} \dots,$

15) $\sum_{k=1}^{\infty} 4^{k-1}$

16) $\sum_{i=1}^{\infty} \left(\frac{1}{3}\right)^{i-1}$

212

Answers of Worksheets – Chapter 21

Arithmetic Sequences

1) First Five Terms: 24, 26, 28, 30, 32, Explicit: $a_n = 22 + 2n$
2) First Five Terms: −15, −20, −25, −30, −35, Explicit: $a_n = -10 - 5n$
3) First Five Terms: 18, 28, 38, 48, 58, Explicit: $a_n = 8 + 10n$
4) First Five Terms: −38, −138, −238, −338, −438, Explicit: $a_n = 62 - 100n$
5) First Five Terms: −31, −38, −45, −52, −59, Explicit: $a_n = -24 - 7n$
6) First Five Terms: −39, −31, −23, −15, −7, Explicit: $a_n = -47 + 8n$
7) First Five Terms: −12.5, −13.6, −14.7, −15.8, −16.9,   Explicit: $a_n = -11.4 - 1.1n$
8) First Five Terms: −21, −51, −81, −111, −141,   Explicit: $a_n = 9 - 30n$
9) Next 3 terms: −46, −48, −50, Recursive: $a_n = a_{n-1} - 2$, $a_1 = -2$
10) Next 3 terms: 30.4, 32.2, 34, Recursive: $a_n = a_{n-1} + 1.8$, $a_1 = 8.8$
11) Next 3 terms: 28.5, 29.6, 30.7, Recursive: $a_n = a_{n-1} + 1.1$, $a_1 = 8.7$
12) Next 3 terms: −0.8, −0.2, 0.4, Recursive: $a_n = a_{n-1} + 0.6$, $a_1 = -13.4$

Geometric Sequences

1) $r = -5$
2) $r = 2$
3) not geometric
4) $r = 5$
5) First Five Terms: 0.8, −4, 20, −100, 500

    Explicit: $a_n = 0.8 \cdot (-5)^{n-1}$

6) First Five Terms: 1, 2, 4, 8, 16

    Explicit: $a_n = 2^{n-1}$

7) Common Ratio: $r = 2$

    First Five Terms: 2, 4, 8, 16. 32

    Explicit: $a_n = 2 \cdot 2^{n-1}$

8) Common Ratio: $r = -3$

    First Five Terms: −3, 9, −27, 81, −243

    Explicit: $a_n = -3 \cdot (-3)^{n-1}$

9) Common Ratio: r = 5

First Five Terms: 2, 10, 50, 250, 1250

Explicit: $a_n = 2 \cdot 5^{n-1}$

10) Common Ratio: r = 3

First Five Terms: $-3, -9, -27, -81, -243$

Explicit: $a_n = -3 \cdot 3^{n-1}$

11) $a_8 = \dfrac{3}{4}$, Recursive: $a_n = a_{n-1} \cdot \dfrac{-1}{2}$, $a_1 = -96$

12) $a_8 = 49152$, Recursive: $a_n = a_{n-1} \cdot 4$, $a_1 = 3$

Comparing Arithmetic and Geometric Sequences

1) Neither
2) Geometric
3) Neither
4) Arithmetic
5) Geometric
6) Arithmetic
7) Neither
8) Arithmetic
9) Arithmetic
10) Arithmetic
11) Geometric
12) Arithmetic
13) Neither
14) Arithmetic
15) Geometric
16) Geometric

Finite Geometric

1) 104
2) −122
3) 51
4) 518
5) 63
6) 52429
7) −19682
8) −130208
9) 13021
10) −1533
11) −170
12) 39364
13) −59048
14) −511

Infinite Geometric

1) Diverges
2) Converges
3) Diverges
4) Converges
5) Converges
6) Diverges
7) $\dfrac{5}{2}$
8) No sum
9) No sum
10) 6
11) 2
12) $\dfrac{243}{4}$
13) 0.625
14) 12
15) No sum
16) $\dfrac{3}{2}$

TSI Test Review

The Texas Success Initiative Assessment, is known as the TSI, is a test to determine the appropriate level of college course work for an incoming student. In essence, it is a broad and quick assessment of students' academic abilities.

The TSI test consists of three separate exams:

- ✓ Mathematics
- ✓ Reading
- ✓ Writing

The mathematics portion of the TSI test contains 20 questions. The test covers data analysis, geometry, and algebra on both intermediate and basic levels.

Students are not allowed to use calculator when taking a TSI assessment. A pop-up calculator is embedded in the test for some questions.

In this section, there are two complete TSI Mathematics Tests. Take these tests to see what score you'll be able to receive on a real TSI test.

Good luck!

TSI Mathematics Practice Tests

Time to Test

Time to refine your skill with a practice examination

Take practice TSI Math Tests to simulate the test day experience. After you've finished, score your tests using the answer keys.

Before You Start

- You'll need a pencil and scratch papers to take the tests.

- After you've finished the test, review the answer key to see where you went wrong.

Mathematics is like love; a simple idea, but it can get complicated.

TSI Mathematics Practice Test 1

(Non–Calculator)

2 Sections – 20 questions

Total time for two sections: No Time Limit

You may NOT use a calculator on this section.

Arithmetic and Elementary Algebra

1) If $1.05 < x \leq 3.04$, then x cannot be equal to:

    A. 3.004

    B. 1.06

    C. 2.07

    D. 3.40

2) What is the area of an isosceles right triangle that has one leg that measures 8 cm?

    A. 28 cm

    B. 32 cm

    C. $8\sqrt{2}$ cm

    D. 72 cm

$\frac{1}{2}(8)(8) = \frac{1}{2}(64) = 32$

3) If two angles in a triangle measure 66 degrees and 42 degrees, what is the value of the third angle?

    A. 24 degrees

    B. 66 degrees

    C. 72 degrees

    D. 108 degrees

4) Which of the following expressions is equivalent to $10 - \frac{2}{3}x \geq 12$

A. $x \geq -3$

B. $x \leq -3$

C. $x \geq 24\frac{1}{3}$

D. $x \leq 24\frac{1}{3}$

$-\frac{2}{3}x \geq 2$

$-2x \geq 6$

$x \leq -3$ when flip by negative

5) Which of the following is a factor of both $x^2 - 2x - 8$ and $x^2 - 6x + 8$?

A. $(x - 4)$

B. $(x + 4)$

C. $(x - 2)$

D. $(x + 2)$

6) $\frac{1}{6b^2} + \frac{1}{6b} = \frac{1}{b^2}$, then $b = $?

common denominator

$1 + b = 6$

$-1 \quad\quad -1$

$b = 5$

A. $-\frac{16}{15}$

B. 5

C. $-\frac{15}{16}$

D. 8

7) $(x + 7)(x + 5) =$

$x^2 + 5x + 7 \cdot 7x + 35$

$x^2 + 12x + 35$

A. $x^2 + 12x + 12$

B. $2x + 12x + 12$

C. $x^2 + 35x + 12$

D. $x^2 + 12x + 35$

8) If x is a positive integer divisible by 6, and $x < 60$, what is the greatest possible value of x?

A. 54

$\frac{54}{6} = 9$

B. 48

C. 36

D. 32

9) $x^2 - 64 = 0$, x could equal to:

A. 6

B. 8

C. 9

D. 32

10) If $a = 8$, what is the value of b in this equation?

$$b = \frac{a^2}{4} + 4$$

A. 24

B. 22

C. 20

D. 18

$\frac{6^4}{4} + 4$

$16 + 4 = 20$

College–Level Mathematics

1) $\tan\left(-\dfrac{\pi}{6}\right) = ?$

tan 30

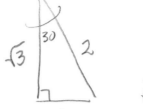

$\dfrac{1 \cdot \sqrt{3}}{\sqrt{3} \cdot \sqrt{3}} = \dfrac{\sqrt{3}}{3}$

   A. $\dfrac{\sqrt{3}}{3}$

   B. $-\dfrac{\sqrt{2}}{2}$

   C. $\dfrac{\sqrt{2}}{2}$

   D. $-\dfrac{\sqrt{3}}{3}$

2) $\dfrac{\sqrt{32\,a^5 b^3}}{\sqrt{2ab^2}} = ?$ $\sqrt{16a^4 b}$ reduce even

   A. $4a^2 \sqrt{b}$

   B. $2b^2 \sqrt{a}$

   C. $4b^2 \sqrt{a}$

   D. $-4a^2 \sqrt{b}$

3) Ella (E) is 4 years older than her friend Ava (A) who is 3 years younger than her sister Sofia (S). If E, A and S denote their ages, which one of the following represents the given information?

A. $\begin{cases} E = A + 4 \\ S = A - 3 \end{cases}$

$A + 4 = E$
$S - 3 = A$

B. $\begin{cases} E = A + 4 \\ A = S + 3 \end{cases}$

$A + 4 = E$
$S - 3 = A$

C. $\begin{cases} A = E + 4 \\ S = A - 3 \end{cases}$

D. $\begin{cases} E = A + 4 \\ A = S - 3 \end{cases}$

4) Which of the following point is the solution of the system of equations?

$$\begin{cases} 5x + y = 9 \\ 10x - 7y = -18 \end{cases}$$

$35x + 7y = 63$
$10x - 7y = -18$
$45x = 45$
$x = 1$

A. (2, 4)

B. (2, 2)

C. (1, 4)

D. (0, 4)

5) Find the Center and Radius of the graph $(x - 3)^2 + (y + 6)^2 = 12$

$x^2 + 9 + y^2 + 36 = \sqrt{12}$
$x^2 + y^2 + 27 = 12$
$-27 \quad -27$
$x^2 + y^2 = -15$

$\sqrt{12}$
$2\sqrt{3}$

A. $(3, 6), \sqrt{3}$

B. $(3, -6), 2\sqrt{3}$

C. $(-3, 6), 2\sqrt{3}$

D. $(3, -6), \sqrt{3}$

6) The cost, in thousands of dollars, of producing x thousands of textbooks is C $(x) = x^2 + 10x + 30$. The revenue, also in thousands of dollars, is R$(x) = 4x$. Find the profit or loss if 3,000 textbooks are produced. (profit = revenue – cost)

A. $21,000 loss

B. $57,000 profit

C. $3,000 profit

D. $57,000 loss

$C(x) = x^2 + 10x + 30$

$4x - (x^2 + 10x + 30)$

$4(3) - (3^2 + 10(3) + 30)$

$12 - 9 - 30 - 30$

$12 - 69$

7) Suppose a triangle has the dimensions indicated below:

Then Sin B = ?

A. $\dfrac{3}{5}$

B. $\dfrac{4}{5}$

C. $\dfrac{4}{3}$

D. $\dfrac{3}{4}$

opposite   hypotenuse

opposite adjacent tan B

adjacent hypotenuse cos

hypotenuse is long
side over 90°
angle

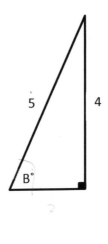

5   4

B°

8) Find the slope–intercept form of the graph $6x - 7y = -12$

A. $y = -\dfrac{7}{6}x - \dfrac{12}{7}$

B. $y = -\dfrac{6}{7}x + 12$

C. $y = \dfrac{6}{7}x + \dfrac{12}{7}$

D. $y = \dfrac{7}{6}x - 12$

$6x - 7y = -12$

$+7y$ $+7y$

$6x = -12 + 7y$

$+12$ $+12$

$\dfrac{12 + 6x}{7} = \dfrac{7y}{7}$

$y = \dfrac{12}{7} + \dfrac{6}{7}x$

9) If $f(x) = 5 + x$ and $g(x) = -x^2 - 1 - 2x$, then find $(g - f)(x)$?

A. $x^2 - 3x - 6$

B. $x^2 - 3x + 6$

C. $-x^2 - 3x + 6$

D. $-x^2 - 3x - 6$

(handwritten work):
$(-x^2 - 1 - 2x) - (5 + x)$
$-5 - x$
$-x^2 - 6 - 3x$

10) $\dfrac{|3+x|}{7} \leq 5$, then $x = ?$

A. $-38 \leq x \leq 35$

B. $-38 \leq x \leq 32$

C. $-32 \leq x \leq 38$

D. $-32 \leq x \leq 32$

(handwritten work):
$7 \cdot \dfrac{|3+x|}{7} \leq 35$
$|3+x| \leq 35$
$-35 \leq 3 + x \leq 35$
$-3 \quad -3 \quad -3$
$-38 \leq x \leq 32$

TSI Mathematics Practice

Test 2

(Non–Calculator)

2 Sections – 20 questions

Total time for two sections: No Time Limit

You may NOT use a calculator on this section.

Arithmetic and Elementary Algebra

1) If $7 + 2x \leq 15$, then $x \leq$?

   A. $14x$

   B. 4

   C. -4

   D. $15x$

2) Last Friday Jacob had $32.52. Over the weekend he received some money for cleaning the attic. He now has $44. How much money did he receive?

   A. $76.52

   B. $11.48

   C. $32.08

   D. $12.58

(handwritten work): 44.00 − 32.52 = 11.48

3) Simplify $\dfrac{\dfrac{1}{2} - \dfrac{x+5}{4}}{\dfrac{x^2}{2} - \dfrac{5}{2}}$

   A. $\dfrac{3-x}{x^2-10}$

   B. $\dfrac{3-x}{2x^2-10}$

   C. $\dfrac{3+x}{x^2-10}$

   D. $\dfrac{-3-x}{2x^2-10}$

(handwritten work):

$\dfrac{\dfrac{2\cdot 1}{2\cdot 2} - \dfrac{x+5}{4}}{\dfrac{x^2-5}{2}}$

$\dfrac{\dfrac{2-(x+5)}{4}}{\dfrac{x^2-5}{2}}$

$-x-3$

$\dfrac{2-x-5}{4} \cdot \dfrac{2}{x^2-5}$

$\dfrac{-x-3}{2x^2-10}$

4) Liam's average (arithmetic mean) on two mathematics tests is 8. What should Liam's score be on the next test to have an overall of 9 for all the tests?

(handwritten) $11 + 16 = \frac{27}{3} = 9$

$\frac{8+8+\_}{3} = 9$

$8+8+\_ = 27$

A. 8

B. 9

C. 10

D. 11 *(circled)*

5) $7^7 \times 7^8 = ?$

A. 7^{56}

B. $7^{0.89}$

C. 7^{15} *(circled)*

D. 1^7

6) What is 5231.48245 rounded to the nearest tenth?

(handwritten) first one

A. 5231.482

B. 5231.5 *(circled)*

C. 5231

D. 5231.48

7) 25 is what percent of 125?

   A. 10%

   B. 20%

   C. 30%

   D. 40%

8) $\sqrt{47}$ is between which two whole numbers?

   A. 3 and 4

   B. 4 and 5

   C. 5 and 6

   D. 6 and 7

9) $(x - 4)(x^2 + 5x + 4) = ?$ $x^3 + 5x^2 + 4x \quad -4x^2 - 20x - 16$

   $$x^3 + x^2 - 16x - 16$$

   A. $x^3 + x^2 - 16x + 16$

   B. $x^3 + 2x^2 - 16x - 16$

   C. $x^3 + x^2 - 16x - 16$

   D. $x^3 + x^2 + 16x - 15$

10) How many 3 × 3 squares can fit inside a rectangle with a height of 54 and width of 12?

A. 72

B. 52

C. 62

D. 42

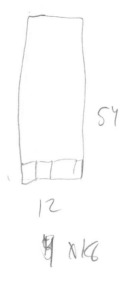

College–Level Mathematics

1) What is cos 30∘?

   A. $\frac{1}{2}$

   B. $\frac{\sqrt{2}}{2}$

   C. $\frac{\sqrt{3}}{2}$

   D. $\sqrt{3}$

2) What's the reciprocal of $\frac{x^3}{16}$?

   A. $\frac{16}{x^3} - 1$

   B. $\frac{48}{x^3}$

   C. $\frac{16}{x^3} + 1$

   D. $\frac{16}{x^3}$

3) If θ is an acute angle and sin θ = $\frac{3}{5}$, then cos θ = ?

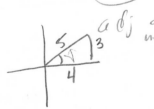

   A. −1

   B. 0

   C. $\frac{4}{5}$

   D. $\frac{5}{4}$

4) What is the solution of the following system of equations?

$$\begin{cases} -2x - y = -9 \\ 5x - 2y = 18 \end{cases}$$

A. (−1, 2)

B. (4, 1)

C. (1, 4)

D. (4, −2)

Handwritten work:
$-2(-2x - y = -9)$
$4x + 2y = 16$
$5x - 2y = 18$
$1x \cdot 0 = 36$

$4x + 2y = 18$
$5x - 2y = 18$
$\overline{\qquad}$
$\dfrac{9x}{9} = \dfrac{36}{9}$
$x = 4$

$5(4) - 2y = 18$
$20 - 2y = 18$
$-20 \qquad -20$
$\dfrac{-2y}{-2} = \dfrac{-2}{-2}$
$y = 1$

5) Solve.

$|9 - (12 \div |2 - 5|)| = ?$

A. 9

B. −6

C. 5

D. −5

Handwritten work:
$|-3|$
absolute value for only negative
psp   3
$12 \div 3 = 4$
$9 - 4$ 18
   5

6) If $\log_2 x = 5$, then $x = ?$

A. 2^{10}

B. $\dfrac{5}{2}$

C. 2^6

D. 32

Handwritten work:
$2^5 = x$
log $\log_2 x = 3$ $2^3 = x$

7) Find the inverse function for ln $(2x + 1)$

A. $\frac{1}{2}(e^x - 1)$

B. $(e^x + 1)$

C. $\frac{1}{2}(e^x + 1)$

D. $(e^x - 1)$

$y = \ln(2x+1)$

$e^x = \cancel{\ln}(2y+1)$

$e^x = 2y + 1$

$e^x - 1 = 2y$

$\frac{1}{2}(e^x - 1) = y$

8) Solve the equation: $\log_4(x + 2) - \log_4(x - 2) = 1$

A. 10

B. $\frac{3}{10}$

C. $\frac{10}{3}$

D. 3

9) Solve $e^{5x + 1} = 10$

A. $\dfrac{\ln(10) + 1}{5}$

B. $\dfrac{\ln(10) - 1}{5}$

C. $5\ln(10) + 2$

D. $5\ln(10) - 2$

10) If $f(x) = x - \dfrac{5}{3}$ and f^{-1} is the inverse of $f(x)$, what is the value of

$f^{-1}(5)$?

A. $\dfrac{10}{3}$

B. $\dfrac{3}{20}$

C. $\dfrac{20}{3}$

D. $\dfrac{3}{10}$

$15 - \dfrac{5}{3}$

$\dfrac{10}{3}$

TSI Mathematics Practice Tests Answers and Explanations

TSI Math Practice Test 1 Answer Key

✳Now, it's time to review your results to see where you went wrong and what areas you need to improve!

Arithmetic and Elementary Algebra

1. D
2. B
3. C
4. B
5. A

6. B
7. D
8. A
9. B
10. C

College–Level Mathematics Test

1. D
2. A
3. D
4. C
5. B

6. D
7. B
8. C
9. D
10. B

TSI Math Practice Test 2 Answer Key

Arithmetic and Elementary Algebra

1. B
2. B
3. D
4. D
5. C

6. B
7. B
8. D
9. C
10. A

College–Level Mathematics Test

1. C
2. D
3. C
4. B
5. C

6. D
7. A
8. C
9. B
10. C

TSI Mathematics Practice Test 1
Answers and Explanations

Arithmetic and Elementary Algebra

1) Choice D is correct

If $1.05 < x \leq 3.04$, then x cannot be equal to 3.40. Because: $3.04 < 3.40$

2) Choice B is correct

$a = 8 \Rightarrow$ area of triangle is $= \frac{1}{2}(8 \times 8) = \frac{64}{2} = 32$ cm

Isosceles right triangle

3) Choice C is correct

$66° + 42° = 108°$

$180° - 108° = 72°$

The value of the third angle is $72°$.

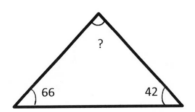

4) Choice B is correct

Simplify:

$10 - \frac{2}{3}x \geq 12 \Rightarrow -\frac{2}{3}x \geq 2 \Rightarrow -x \geq 3 \Rightarrow x \leq -3$

5) Choice A is correct

Factor each trinomial $x^2 - 2x - 8$ and $x^2 - 6x + 8$

$x^2 - 2x - 8 \Rightarrow (x - 4)(x + 2)$

$x^2 - 6x + 8 \Rightarrow (x - 2)(x - 4)$

$(x - 4)$ is a factor of both trinomial.

6) Choice B is correct

$\dfrac{1 + b}{6b^2} = \dfrac{1}{b^2} \Rightarrow (b \neq 0)\ b^2 + b^3 = 6b^2 \Rightarrow b^3 - 5b^2 = 0 \Rightarrow b^2(b - 5) = 0 \Rightarrow b - 5 = 0 \Rightarrow b = 5$

7) Choice D is correct

Use FOIL (First, Out, In, Last)

$(x + 7)(x + 5) = x^2 + 5x + 7x + 35 = x^2 + 12x + 35$

8) Choice A is correct

$\dfrac{54}{6} = \dfrac{27}{3} = 9, \quad \dfrac{48}{6} = \dfrac{24}{3} = 8, \quad \dfrac{36}{6} = \dfrac{18}{3} = 6, \quad \dfrac{59}{6} = \dfrac{59}{6} \qquad$ 59 is prime number

The answer is 54.

9) Choice B is correct

$x^2 - 64 = 0 \Rightarrow x^2 = 64 \Rightarrow x = 8$

10) Choice C is correct

If $a = 8$ then $b = \dfrac{8^2}{4} + 4 \Rightarrow b = \dfrac{64}{4} + 4 \Rightarrow b = 16 + 4 = 20$

College–Level Mathematics

1) Choice D is correct

$$\tan\left(-\frac{\pi}{6}\right) = -\frac{\sqrt{3}}{3}$$

2) Choice A is correct

$$\frac{\sqrt{32a^5b^3}}{\sqrt{2ab^2}} = \frac{4a^2b\sqrt{2ab}}{b\sqrt{2a}} = 4a^2\sqrt{b}$$

3) Choice D is correct

E = 4 + A

A = S − 3

4) Choice C is correct

$$\begin{cases} 5x + y = 9 \\ 10x - 7y = -18 \end{cases} \Rightarrow \text{Multiplication } (-2) \text{ in first equation} \Rightarrow \begin{cases} -10x - 2y = -18 \\ 10x - 7y = -18 \end{cases}$$

Add two equations together $\Rightarrow -9y = -36 \Rightarrow y = 4$ then: $x = 1$

5) Choice B is correct

$(x - h)^2 + (y - k)^2 = r^2 \Rightarrow$ center: (h, k) and radius: r

$(x - 3)^2 + (y + 6)^2 = 12 \Rightarrow$ center: $(3, -6)$ and radius: $2\sqrt{3}$

6) Choice D is correct

$c(3) = (3)^2 + 10(3) + 30 = 9 + 30 + 30 = 69$

$4 \times 3 = 12 \Rightarrow 12 - 69 = -57 \Rightarrow 57,000 \text{ loss}$

7) Choice B is correct

$$\sin B = \frac{\text{the length of the side that is opposite that angle}}{\text{the length of the longest side of the triangle}} = \frac{4}{5}$$

8) Choice C is correct

$$-7y = -6x - 12 \Rightarrow y = \frac{-6}{-7}x - \frac{12}{-7} \Rightarrow y = \frac{6}{7}x + \frac{12}{7}$$

9) Choice D is correct

$$(g - f)(x) = g(x) - f(x) = (-x^2 - 1 - 2x) - (5 + x)$$

$$-x^2 - 1 - 2x - 5 - x = -x^2 - 3x - 6$$

10) Choice B is correct

$$\frac{|3 + x|}{7} \leq 5 \Rightarrow |3 + x| \leq 35 \Rightarrow -35 \leq 3 + x \leq 35 \Rightarrow -35 - 3 \leq x \leq 35 - 3 \Rightarrow$$

$$-38 \leq x \leq 32$$

TSI Mathematics Practice Test 2
Answers and Explanations

Arithmetic and Elementary Algebra

1) Choice B is correct

Simplify:

$7 + 2x \leq 15 \Rightarrow 2x \leq 15 - 7 \Rightarrow 2x \leq 8 \Rightarrow x \leq 4$

2) Choice B is correct

$\$44 - \$32.52 = \$11.48$

3) Choice D is correct

Simplify:

$$\frac{\dfrac{1}{2} - \dfrac{x+5}{4}}{\dfrac{x^2}{2} - \dfrac{5}{2}} = \frac{\dfrac{1}{2} - \dfrac{x+5}{4}}{\dfrac{x^2 - 5}{2}} = \frac{2\left(\dfrac{1}{2} - \dfrac{x+5}{4}\right)}{x^2 - 5}$$

$\Rightarrow$Simplify: $\dfrac{1}{2} - \dfrac{x+5}{4} = \dfrac{-x-3}{4}$

then: $\dfrac{2\left(\dfrac{-x-3}{4}\right)}{x^2 - 5} = \dfrac{\dfrac{-x-3}{2}}{x^2 - 5} = \dfrac{-x-3}{2(x^2 - 5)} = \dfrac{-x-3}{2x^2 - 10}$

4) Choice D is correct

$$\frac{a+b}{2} = 8 \qquad \Rightarrow \qquad a + b = 16$$

$$\frac{a+b+c}{3} = 9 \qquad \Rightarrow \qquad a + b + c = 27$$

$$16 + c = 27 \qquad \Rightarrow \qquad c = 27 - 16 = 11$$

5) Choice C is correct

$7^7 \times 7^8 = 7^{7+8} = 7^{15}$

6) Choice B is correct

Underline the tenth place:

5231.$\underline{4}$8245

Look to the right if it is 5 or above, give it a shove.

Then, round up to 5231.5

7) Choice B is correct

$$125 \times \frac{x}{100} = 25 \qquad \Rightarrow \qquad 75 \times x = 1500 \qquad \Rightarrow \qquad x = \frac{1500}{75} = 20$$

8) Choice D is correct

$\sqrt{47} = 6.85565...$

then: $\sqrt{47}$ is between 6 and 7

9) Choice C is correct

Use FOIL (First, Out, In, Last)

$(x - 4)(x^2 + 5x + 4) = x^3 + 5x^2 + 4x - 4x^2 - 20x - 16$

$= x^3 + x^2 - 16x - 16$

10) Choice A is correct

Number of squares equal to: $\frac{54 \times 12}{3 \times 3} = 18 \times 4 = 72$

College–Level Mathematics Test

1) Choice C is correct

$cos\ 30° = \frac{\sqrt{3}}{2}$

2) Choice D is correct

$\frac{x^3}{16}$ $\quad \Rightarrow$ reciprocal is : $\frac{16}{x^3}$

3) Choice C is correct

$sin\theta = \frac{3}{5} \Rightarrow$ we have following triangle, then

$c = \sqrt{5^2 - 3^2} = \sqrt{25 - 9} = \sqrt{16} = 4$

$cos\theta = \frac{4}{5}$

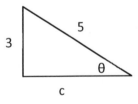

4) Choice B is correct

$$\begin{cases} -2x - y = -9 \\ 5x - 2y = 18 \end{cases} \Rightarrow \text{Multiplication } (-2) \text{ in first equation} \Rightarrow \begin{cases} 4x + 2y = 18 \\ 5x - 2y = 18 \end{cases}$$

Add two equations together $\Rightarrow 9x = 36 \Rightarrow x = 4$ then: $y = 1$

5) Choice C is correct

$|9 - (12 \div |\, 2 - 5\, |)| = |9 - (12 \div |-3|)| = |9 - (12 \div 3)| = |9 - 4| = |5| = 5$

6) Choice D is correct

<u>METHOD ONE</u>

$\log_2 x = 5$

Apply logarithm rule: $a = \log_b(b^a)$

$5 = \log_2(2^5) = \log_2(32)$

$\log_2 x = \log_2(32)$

When the logs have the same base: $\log_b(f(x)) = \log_b(g(x)) \Rightarrow f(x) = g(x)$

then: $x = 32$

<u>METHOD TWO</u>

We know that: $\qquad \log_a b = c \Rightarrow b = a^c \qquad \log_2 x = 5 \Rightarrow x = 2^5 = 32$

7) Choice A is correct

$f(x) = \ln(2x + 1)$

$y = \ln(2x + 1)$

Change variables x and y: $x = \ln(2y + 1)$

solve: $x = \ln(2y + 1)$

$y = \dfrac{e^x - 1}{2} = \dfrac{1}{2}(e^x - 1)$

8) Choice C is correct

<u>METHOD ONE</u>

$\log_4(x + 2) - \log_4(x - 2) = 1$

Add $\log_4(x - 2)$ to both sides

$\log_4(x + 2) - \log_4(x - 2) + \log_4(x - 2) = 1 + \log_4(x - 2)$

$\log_4(x + 2) = 1 + \log_4(x - 2)$

Apply logarithm rule: $a = \log_b(b^a) \Rightarrow 1 = \log_4(4^1) = \log_4(4)$

then: $\log_4(x + 2) = \log_4(4) + \log_4(x - 2)$

Logarithm rule: $\log_c(a) + \log_c(b) = \log_c(ab)$

then: $\log_4(4) + \log_4(x - 2) = \log_4(4(x - 2))$

$\log_4(x + 2) = \log_4(4(x - 2))$

When the logs have the same base: $\log_b(f(x)) = \log_b(g(x)) \Rightarrow f(x) = g(x)$

$(x + 2) = 4(x - 2)$

$x = \dfrac{10}{3}$

<u>METHOD TWO</u>

We know that: $\quad \log_a b - \log_a c = \log_a \dfrac{b}{c} \quad$ and $\quad \log_a b = c \Rightarrow b = a^c$

Then: $\log_4(x + 2) - \log_4(x - 2) = \log_4 \dfrac{x+2}{x-2} = 1 \Rightarrow \dfrac{x+2}{x-2} = 4^1 = 4 \Rightarrow x + 2 = 4(x - 2)$

$\Rightarrow x + 2 = 4x - 8 \Rightarrow 4x - x = 8 + 2 \rightarrow 3x = 10 \Rightarrow x = \dfrac{10}{3}$

9) Choice B is correct

$e^{5x + 1} = 10$

If $f(x) = g(x)$, then $\ln(f(x)) = \ln(g(x))$

$\ln(e^{5x + 1}) = \ln(10)$

Apply logarithm rule: $\log_a(x^b) = b\log_a(x)$

$\ln(e^{5x + 1}) = (5x + 1)\ln(e)$

$(5x + 1)\ln(e) = \ln(10)$

$(5x + 1)\ln(e) = (5x + 1)$

$(5x + 1) = \ln(10) \qquad\Rightarrow\qquad x = \dfrac{\ln(10) - 1}{5}$

10) Choice C is correct

$f(x) = x - \dfrac{5}{3} \quad\Rightarrow\quad y = x - \dfrac{5}{3} \Rightarrow \quad y + \dfrac{5}{3} = x$

$f^{-1} = x + \dfrac{5}{3}$

$f^{-1}(5) = 5 + \dfrac{5}{3} = \dfrac{20}{3}$

"Effortless Math" Publications

Effortless Math authors' team strives to prepare and publish the best quality Mathematics learning resources to make learning Math easier for all. We hope that our publications help you or your student Math in an effective way.

We all in Effortless Math wish you good luck and successful studies!

Effortless Math Authors

www.EffortlessMath.com

... So Much More Online!

✓ FREE Math lessons

✓ More Math learning books!

✓ Mathematics Worksheets

✓ Online Math Tutors

Need a PDF version of this book?

Please visit www.EffortlessMath.com

Made in the USA
Lexington, KY
30 March 2019